What people are saying about…

OVERCOMING
Mediocrity©

5 out of 5 Stars
Very Inspiring!

"It is so great hearing how these women have not stopped in the face of life happening. In these times, this is needed more than ever. A great read for those who are looking to empower other women."

—Lauren

5 out of 5 Stars
Wonderful Motivational Book! So Inspiring!

Wonderful motivational book! Very uplifting stories. I bought a couple for my Christmas and birthday presents!"

—Ericka

5 out of 5 Stars
Fearlessly and Wonderfully Made!

"This book is so encouraging and uplifting I couldn't put it down. I originally got this book to support one of my dear friends but quickly fell in love with every story that I read. The encouragement that came from every story hit in every aspect of my life. I'm so grateful something like this was written. The younger generation definitely needs to hear stories and successful stories of women that suffer through some hard times and come out victorious!!"

—Eden

5 out of 5 Stars
Excellent Read for Men and Women!

"LOVED THE BOOK! [Husband] thought it should not be limited to a "women's" book — excellent for men and women. Writing was personal, intimate, yet clearly educational in nature. Long enough to take you somewhere, but short enough to sit down and read right then. The book is downloaded on our Kindle, so we can read again."

—TJ

5 out of 5 Stars
Very Inspiring!

"Thank you, ladies, for telling your stories. So inspiring, love the book. Bought multiple copies to give to my girlfriends that are unstoppable woman in my life. Thank you."

—Julie

5 out of 5 Stars
Highly Recommend!!

"HIGHLY RECOMMEND!!! If you are looking for personal and professional development, this book is for you! It is perfectly inspiring, educational, empowering, and beautifully written! I could really relate to the struggles in their personal stories and it has helped me to continue working on overcoming my own obstacles so I can succeed in life and in business! Thank you all for sharing your incredible journeys."

—Lisa

5 out of 5 Stars
Uplifting and Inspirational!

"Very inspiring, powerful book! Love women supporting women! Would highly recommend!"

—Amazon Reviewer

5 out of 5 Stars

It's a Great Investment in Yourself!

"This is an inspiring compilation. Each woman's story contains powerful lessons that are widely applicable. Heartwarming and triumphant all at the same time. Any woman who's tread a rocky path on her life's journey will be able to relate and rejoice along with each author as she overcomes adversity and challenge. If you're seeking inspiration to overcome adversity, take a moment to breathe, regroup, and soak up a story or three. It's a great investment in yourself."

—Debbra

What our clients are saying about…

OVERCOMING
Mediocrity©

"If you're on the fence, I'd highly recommend and encourage you to jump in feet first because not only did I get to work with other amazing women, but I also ended up being an Amazon Bestselling Author which is a huge boost for my career and brand. I hope that you'll choose to share your inspiring story for all of the many women who are going to read it."

—Amber Champagne-Matos
Founder of Champagne Apothecary
Overcoming Mediocrity Unstoppable Women

"I'm passionate about helping women overcome the lies that are holding them back. The problem was that I still believed my own lies. I questioned if my story could actually make a difference, feared that no one would want to hear it and didn't trust I could write it well enough for it to be published. Until I met Christie. She invited me to share my story in one of her books, and it completely transformed my business, my life and best of all, the lives of the women who read it. They've reached out to me, grateful for how what I shared helped them overcome their adversities. Hearing those women's testimonies gave me confidence and fueled me to keep writing. With Christie's help, I published my own book just a few months later, and am currently writing the next in that series."

—Shannon Ferraby
Author, Speaker, and Trainer with Success Unwrapped
Overcoming Mediocrity Influential Women

"Being a part of this book made such a difference and I love the conversations that Christie and I had together. They were so rich and revealing that I actually can do a TED talk. But really, what really broke through for me is being able to share my story and to be a subject expert. Since then, I've been on other people's podcasts and I started my own podcast 'Tea Time Midlife Edition.' If you have a story that you want to share with the world, get in front of Christie."

—Regina Young
Podcaster and CEO of Modelperfect Woman
Overcoming Mediocrity Unstoppable Women

"Being an Amazon Bestselling Author alongside some fabulous women in this series has propelled me forward in ways that I wouldn't have had otherwise. I've since guested on podcasts, I have an episode on Amazon Fire TV, and I've had so many women tell me how inspired they've been by the book. Secondarily, I was able to tell my story in a really authentic way and not have it completely rearranged in the editing process. I'm really excited to see what the future holds."

—Tiffany Lewis
CEO of More Meaningful Marketing
Overcoming Mediocrity Unstoppable Women

"Christie Ruffino is a master at taking women's women who are passionate about telling their story, but they don't know exactly how they're going to do it and molding us into not only authors but Amazon Bestselling Authors. It was an amazing six-month journey, where I got to meet some amazing women, discover their stories, and realize that what I have to say is important and something that the world needs to hear."

—Danica Joan
Founder of Kids Need Both, Inc
Overcoming Mediocrity Unstoppable Women

"Me, an Amazon number one Bestselling Author. What a crazy exciting journey this has been and an accomplishment I would have never dreamed of. Joining the Overcoming Mediocrity project has brought me so many new connections, as well as the credibility and the credentials for my business. Becoming an author is something I never planned to do in my lifetime but has been a very, very exciting ride!"

—Laura Fank-Carrara
President of Laura Ocean Solutions
Overcoming Mediocrity Unstoppable Women

"Being an author in the series has opened doors for me. It makes it easier to rise to the top of the list for those responsible for booking speaking gigs to want to talk to me. The traffic to my website and Business Page has increased measurably. It has shortened the know, like, trust factor. People are reaching out to me first before I reach out to them. The titles of the books help women who want to stretch themselves. Who wouldn't want to associate themselves and work with an author who is Dynamic, Resilient, Strong, and Influential?"

—Jeanne Lyons
Career Breakthrough Coach
Overcoming Mediocrity Influential Women

"Working with Christie and her team was just the nudge I needed to finally sit down and start writing. The social media tips that were provided when the book launched were also invaluable for engaging and re-engaging people who follow me. I am much more confident about my next book and its launch."

—Valerie Mrak
Speaker • Filmmaker • Storyteller • Coach
Overcoming Mediocrity Victorious Women

"Christie and the OM team took an overwhelming and complicated process of book publishing and made it very easy to get my story published. I was guided through the process from start to finish. Every detail was outlined, and my questions were always answered promptly. The book has received rave reviews, and it has taken my credibility to the next level, as I am now an Amazon #1 best seller! Thank you!!"

—Lynn O'Dowd
Motivational Speaker and Keynote Performer
Overcoming Mediocrity Influential Women

"When I learned about this project, I was already fully into the writing, publishing, and marketing process of my other book, *Getting Yourself Unstuck*. However, I couldn't put everything in that book. Therefore, *Overcoming Mediocrity* allowed me to publish a very personal story that didn't seem to fit in my other book. Now going forward in my marketing, the two books will work in tandem."

—Angie Engstrom
Coach and Plank Trainer
Overcoming Mediocrity Resilient Women

OVERCOMING MEDIOCRITY

Other Overcoming Mediocrity Titles

Overcoming Mediocrity — Dynamic Women

Overcoming Mediocrity — Courageous Women

Overcoming Mediocrity — Strong Women

Overcoming Mediocrity — Remarkable Women

Overcoming Mediocrity — Resilient Women

Overcoming Mediocrity — Influential Women

Overcoming Mediocrity — Victorious Women

Overcoming Mediocrity — Fearless Women

Overcoming Mediocrity — Unstoppable Women

EMPOWERED WOMEN
OVERCOMING
Mediocrity©

A unique collection of stories from empowered women who have created their own lives of significance!

Presented by Christie L. Ruffino

DPWN Publishing

www.OvercomingMediocrity.org

For more information, contact:
DPWN Publishing
A division of the Dynamic Professional Women's Network, Inc.
1879 N. Neltnor Blvd. #316, West Chicago, IL 60185
www.OvercomingMediocrity.org
www.OurDPWN.com

Printed in the United States of America

ISBN: 978-1-939794-21-5

Dedication

This book is dedicated to the eighteen empowered women whose stories are in this book and the countless women whose are not. They all bravely faced and overcame challenging times during an unprecedented time in human history; the 2020/2021 COVID-19 epidemic.

A special dedication to the most EMPOWERED woman in my life, Susan Jean Giannini (Crowley). Sue was my best friend, my confidant, my advisor, my encourager, my number one fan, and my beloved mom. Although she couldn't overcome the debilitating physical conditions that plagued her final years, she demonstrated courage and sheer unstoppableness during every aspect of her life until the very end. Not even a year has passed since she left, but I can feel her presence every day and know she is still my biggest cheerleader.

You can read her story in the *Overcoming Mediocrity — Remarkable Women* book and at www.MyLegacyJournal.com/Sue

The Power of a Story

There is nothing more important in this world than the relationships we build and the legacy we leave in the lives of those who've crossed paths with us on our journey of life. It's the experiences we have during this journey that define our individual uniqueness and create our own powerful personal blueprint or our unique story snowflake.

It is this blueprint that can empower and equip us to possess a distinct advantage over every other person in this world, if leveraged correctly and shared. If we don't have the courage to share our snowflake, it will be lost forever. No one will have the same story, and no one can repeat your story. Therefore, those who come after you will never learn anything from what you've experienced and what you've learned.

I feel that the most significant thing we can do to add value back to this world, is to master the narrative of our lives. All of our leadership and moneymaking abilities rest in our ability to discover, craft, and deliver our personal story or message in a way that will allow people to connect to us. The right story shared at the right time with the right person can alter the trajectory of their life, as well as our own.

We can also learn from other people's stories to change the direction of our own story and redirect our ultimate destiny.

Power to you and the story of your life!

"Challenges are our opportunity to train for a greater purpose.

Faced with trouble, some people grow wings;

others buy crutches. Which person are you?"

—Christie Ruffino

Introduction

When I embarked upon this journey, never in my wildest dreams did I expect it to turn out as it has. My motives were grand, yet much more simplistic than they are today.

My initial goal was to create one co-authored book, collecting stories from women I admired who were members of my organization, the Dynamic Professional Women's Network (DPWN). I knew how sharing my story in a similar book (compiled by a mentor of mine, Michelle Prince) had been transformational for me. I also knew how having a book to share in the business community gave me additional credibility, recognition, and exposure. What I didn't know was how these same stories would be just as transformational for the readers, as they related with one or more of the women who were willing to share their stories in such a vulnerable and authentic way.

I also had no way of knowing how working with these women would lead me down a path that would change "my" life forever…

My Story

I'm a natural connector. Many women are. I believe it's part of our DNA to connect people with other people or resources that can help them. I've often shared how my journey to build DPWN was not intentional. As an introvert, the last thing I wanted to do was build a business where I would have to frequently talk with new people…strangers. But thankfully, God knew better than I did what was best for me.

Now, 18 years later, our community is thriving in the Chicagoland area, and we've expanded globally. We have a fierce online presence with virtual meetings, on-demand training, and Mastermind Success Circles. You can connect with us at www.OurDPWN.com.

I personally work with women who are on a quest to build a profitable purpose-driven business as a coach, author, and speaker. That is my passion and where my story has brought me thus far. I'm blessed to wake up every day, knowing that I can help my clients live into THEIR passion; which is to help their clients. We're creating a wonderful ripple effect. You can connect with me at www.ChristieRuffino.com.

Our *Overcoming Mediocrity Project* is going just as strong, celebrating book number ten featuring an amazing lineup of empowered women and a brand-new Podcast. The stories in each of our books are about strength, faith, and courage. They are about having the confidence to believe in ourselves, even when those we love may not. They're about having the courage to do hard things, even when we don't want to. And they're about remaining empowered through all of life's ups and downs because that is what, as women, we do brilliantly. Do you have a story of strength, faith, or courage? You can connect with us at www.OvercomingMediocrity.org.

Your Story

What is your story? ARE YOU LIVING YOUR STORY? Or are you living for someone else's story? Maybe you ARE living into your destiny. Or maybe you spend the majority of your time unhappily working for someone else, taking care of someone else, or doing something that does not create a fire in your soul. You're managing, thinking…one of these days it will be my turn. What if that time never comes?

The personal and professional development industry generates billions of dollars of revenue every year. According to www.marketresearch.com, the U.S. estimated market value for personal coaching was $955 million in 2015 and $1.02 billion in 2016. This market value is expected to reach $1.34 billion by 2022 which is a 6.7% average yearly growth rate.

The great news is that for every one of those coaches, there are countless people desperately searching for help.

I work with women who have reached a point in their lives, where they're finally ready to step into their destiny, own their story, and share their wisdom. Women who don't think they have the skills to become a coach, but they know down deep in their gut that they can help people. They're considering stepping into a coaching or consulting role, but they don't know where to start, or they've been trying, and they're just not getting the results they desire (or frankly that they deserve).

If you just read that and felt a butterfly or two swirling around in your stomach, then maybe we should chat. I have a simple system that will provide you with the steps and support to build a profitable business as a coach, author, and speaker.

Our Books — Their Story

Our first *Overcoming Mediocrity* book was a smashing success! On the very first day of its release in 2013, it became the #1 downloaded Kindle book in the motivational genre category. Twenty-two women shared their stories to inspire other women to overcome and succeed as they had, and all authors were able to claim the distinguished Amazon Bestselling Author status.

Because of the overwhelming success of that first book, we went on to produce additional books under the *Overcoming Mediocrity* brand. Each of them also climbed to the #1 position on Amazon on the very first day of release. Three of them, *Overcoming Mediocrity — Resilient Women, Influential Women,* and *Fearless Women*, all reached the #1 position in two categories which was a great accomplishment.

These books have ultimately taken on a life of their own and have made a greater impact than ever anticipated. It is exciting to read testimonials from women who have read and connected with one or more of the inspirational stories inside. It's even more exciting when one of those same women decide to share their story in one of our future books.

It is now with great honor and pride that I can share stories from the empowered women in this book. I've had the pleasure of getting to know each of these ladies and learning about the stories they're sharing with you. I'm deeply inspired by the courage they're exhibiting. They are sharing the personal details of their lives with the sole intention of allowing you, the reader, to learn from their experiences and wisdom.

It's easy to become complacent. Live a life of mediocrity, just coasting through day by day. It takes courage to fight through the hard and overcome challenges that seem impossible to defeat. The women in the pages of this book made a purposeful choice to live significant lives and share their stories to help you also live a life of significance. This demonstrates strength, humility, and the heart of a true go-giver. These women all have even greater things yet to come. They are women whom you should know, learn from, and emulate.

This book is meant to not only encourage you but to also awaken your inner desire to share your story along with them. Each woman in our project wants to make the biggest possible impact in the world and transform as many lives as possible, by sharing their story and wisdom in a book that will get massive exposure. They could have kept their stories private. That would have been the safest and easiest path for them. However, they decided to step out of their comfort zone and share the narratives of their lives with you. We invite you to join them on this journey.

I am blessed to have the opportunity to share these EMPOWERED women with you. I hope you feel just as blessed to receive the value they offer you.

Hugs & Blessings,

Christie

Table of Contents

Lauren Bergiel

Mining for Gold

The Moment Everything Changed.

The sun is shining brightly through the brisk, cold January air. I'm in the car, bopping my head, singing without restraint: "Don't worry about a thing, 'Cause every little thing gonna be all riiiight!" The song is Bob Marley's "Three Little Birds." My happy anthem. I am free as a bird. I planned this solo road trip from Chicago to Florida well over a year ago, and NOW I am finally doing it! I enjoy traveling by myself. There is something about the ability to go wherever I want, whenever I want. I am looking forward to being in the sunshine state, but first, I have a few fun, adventurous stops planned along the way!

While driving, I think back to a week ago, when I went in for a routine mammogram. The doctors had advised me to go for a biopsy because they saw something odd. Doctors were always cautious with me because breast cancer is prevalent on my mother's side of the family. I figured it was probably nothing to worry about since all previous scares were false alarms. It was still better to know for sure.

With Nashville now in the rearview mirror, I set course for Atlanta. Fun memories of the past weekend dance in my head until my phone rings, abruptly interrupting my hazy daydream. I quickly glance at the phone and recognize the number. It is my doctor. Relieved for his call, I wait to hear the official news that this is, yet again, nothing to worry about. Usually, his voice is warm and inviting. This time, however, he sounds a little more matter-of-fact. The next thing he declares sends shockwaves through my body as if hit by lightning: *"It's Cancer."*

My stomach drops, my chest tightens, and my throat feels as dry as a desert. For once in my life, I am speechless. The expressway begins to blur around me. These are the last words I am expecting to hear at age 33. My eyes hold back their tears. I planned this amazing trip for the past year, and I haven't even made it to my final destination. *Do I turn around now and go home? What am I supposed to do??*

I finally gather up some strength and mutter back to my doctor, "Sh-h-hould, I just turn around and drive back home?" He explains that it is a slow-growing tumor, and another week or two would not significantly impact the outcome (*whatever that might be*). He recommends that I complete my trip and tells me that we will discuss a course of action when I return home. We say our goodbyes and hang up. Translating his unspoken words, I heard him say that I better have fun and enjoy this road trip because the other road ahead would be anything but fun and easy. *But how could I enjoy my journey with this dark news hanging over my head?*

It's Cancer. Those two words rocked my entire universe. Inside the car, silence enveloped me. I felt a barrage of thoughts rush into my mind, like water breaching a dam. I was in my early 30's. Single, not married. No children. *Did I even want children? Could I still have them if I did want them? How would that work? Did I have to decide this now?? Would I have to have chemotherapy? Surgery? What was going to happen to me? Would I live? Would I die? What was going to happen to my hair? My breasts? What would happen to the business that I worked so hard all of these years to build? How would my parents and family take this news?* I knew for sure this would break their hearts. The line of questioning continued to bombard my mind for hours until I finally arrived at my hotel in Atlanta. My head was throbbing, but the rest of my body was numb. On autopilot, I managed to eat. Soon after dinner, I laid down in bed exhausted. I had one final realization before I drifted off to sleep: Life would never be the same from this point on.

Decisions, Decisions!

Weeks later, I was back in Chicago, inundated with doctor appointments. I learned that I could have the lump in my breast removed, have one breast removed, or opt for both breasts to be removed. Understanding the gravity of the decision, I opted for a double mastectomy. It was not easy, but I knew without a doubt that would be the course I would take. *How did I know without a doubt?* I was aware of a very clear and confident voice deep down within me telling me so. While cancer was only found in one breast, my age and family history meant I remained at high risk for future recurrence. If I would survive this experience, I wanted to reduce the possibility of recurrence as much as I could.

Although it was highly recommended, I hadn't fully come to terms with chemotherapy. What doctors don't like to tell you is that chemotherapy, in itself, is carcinogenic. That scared the hell out of me. That same crystal clear voice that I relied on for earlier decisions was nowhere to be found on this matter. I did know that I would first need to explore natural modalities before moving forward with my decision.

I went down an informational rabbit hole, learning about the human body as an ecosystem. How it operates, what throws it off, and how to get it back in balance. I learned how nutrition, stress, and toxins affect the body. I wanted very badly to believe there was a natural route that could provide evidence of erasing cancer. I tirelessly read articles and books and watched countless videos. I spoke to oncologists, medical doctors, acupuncturists, naturopathic doctors, holistic healers, and nutritionists. There was no shortage of opinions, and they were very polarized. I searched high and low for data on natural alternatives but came up empty-handed. At that time, there was no significant research done on natural remedies affecting cancer, and the instances that gave some indication of success for alternative treatments were primarily anecdotal. I spent many nights crying from frustration. *How could there be no reliable testing and research on natural remedies and cancer?*

I was desperate, so I traveled to San Diego to meet a supportive friend who would go to Mexico with me to a healing center that touted their natural remedies. I crossed the border with skepticism yet remained hopeful that a possible alternative would be revealed. I was close to considering their methods — until, in the lobby of the doctor's office, I saw a historical video on the doctor who created the center. It turns out he died of cancer. *Go figure.*

I was deeply confused. I just couldn't seem to connect with that clear voice inside that usually knew the answers. Debating whether to do chemotherapy or alternative natural methods, I made arguments for both and flip-flopped every minute. Trapped in a vicious cycle of doubt, I feared the choice could cost me my life. *What if I chose wrong??* I needed to choose powerfully so that I could move forward and stand confidently behind my choice, no matter the outcome. I still had NO idea what I wanted to do, but I knew that I couldn't prolong this anymore. I felt the weight of the pressure to make a decision, and it drained my energy.

In San Diego, I continued feverishly absorbing information, believing that the choice would reveal itself to me with more knowledge. Unfortunately, the more information I consumed, the more confused I became. My friend, an experienced nurse, could tell that I was at the end of my mental capacity, so she took me to watch the sunset. She turned to me and said, "You will never have all the information in the world. Even then, the choice may still not be clear. All you can do is take the information you do have and choose a path that resonates most with you at this time. Stand behind that choice…whether you live or die. Doing otherwise will only give you unneeded stress." She hugged me, and I cried. On our way home, I let what she said sink in.

Later that evening, the words of my friend still echoed through me. I closed my eyes and quieted my mind. I was determined to connect with that all-knowing voice inside of me which had been so quiet. After an hour of being still, I finally heard it say, *"I wish there were more proof regarding natural modalities working against cancer. However, we haven't found any substantial information. There seems to be a lot of empirical data that chemotherapy works to extend your life, even if there are short-term and possible long-term implications. Although this isn't what you want to hear, chemotherapy seems like the best course of action given the information you have now."*

While the choice to receive chemotherapy won out only by a tiny margin, that was what there was for me to do. In reality, I could not know the "right" way in that moment or any moment for that matter. We never know if something works out the way we want it to until we have the perspective to look back. All we can do is choose the "best" way, which is the way that resonates and aligns most at that moment in time, even if it's only slightly more.

Tears flowed freely down my face as if a faucet had been turned on. Carrying around the stress of a life-or-death decision is like holding a 500-pound tiger. It was a relief to set that weight down finally. Powerfully making that choice allowed me to take action and set up the necessary appointments to move forward.

It's Okay to Not Be Okay...

Shortly after I was diagnosed, I learned that even with insurance, cancer treatment is expensive. There are many out-of-pocket expenses. One of my closest friends asked if she could put together a fundraiser to help pay for my medical expenses. I was so conflicted! Not only would people find out about my diagnosis, but I was also going to ask for their money?! *I didn't want to take other people's money! I didn't want others to think I was weak. I didn't want others to believe that something was wrong with me or see me as a woman with cancer.* Raised as an independent woman, I was never good at asking others for help. However, my friend convinced me that it was okay to accept financial support from others and that some people would naturally want to express their love that way.

Nonetheless, when my friend published the fundraiser on Facebook, my heart sank. The world would now know everything! Gulp! It was an incredibly humbling moment. Then something miraculous happened. Hundreds of people began sharing encouraging messages. Many people donated money without hesitation. I was overwhelmed by the amount of love and support that people gave. Never in a million years did I imagine people would show up the way they did.

Compelled to give back, I gave authentically of myself. I posted weekly videos of my journey. I showed the most vulnerable parts of myself, which included showing my unsightly surgical port, chopping off my hair, cancer treatments, and my Ms. Clean bald head, as well as other struggles, including times when I cried. I mean, this was real life. Why cover it up? People walk around every day, putting on a happy face and pretending that everything is okay, yet it hardly ever is. I didn't see any value in complaining, but I was not covering up the difficulties I was facing either.

Sharing my journey, in turn, further inspired others to give in creative ways. People painted pictures, sent books, cards, and other uplifting gifts and care packages. These always seemed to arrive just when I needed it most. Some people continued to donate money. Others donated venues for fundraisers. I was offered photo shoots, dance lessons, and haircuts at no charge. Another friend donated his time to organize a second fundraiser, where I walked fiercely down the runway bald, wearing a fabulous red gown and pink boxing gloves!

Looking back, I realize that what sparked this exchange was my own willingness to be vulnerable. I was okay with not being okay and allowing others to help me. By sharing my journey with others and accepting their support, I was able to focus on my daily life without financial worry. Many commented how much of an inspiration I was to them during this time. Knowing I contributed to others just as much as I got from their love and support felt like a win!

The Only Thing I Can Truly Control.

I remember feeling like I didn't have much control over anything during this period of my life. Cancer stripped away all of the things I enjoyed.

Everything I knew about myself quickly faded. Luckily, I had the sense that there was still *one* thing I had control over…*my mind.*

I read a lot about the power of the "now" moment and practicing gratitude. Although I understood it in theory, I was not an expert at practicing either concept. I certainly had no idea how to be thankful, given my current set of circumstances. From where I was standing, someone might as well have asked me to leap over the Grand Canyon. I knew I needed support, so I recruited a good friend to hold me accountable. We agreed to send each other a list of ten things we were thankful for every day. We did this for months.

Then one day, I was sitting around the pool with my parents. Things became more vibrant than usual. I felt the energizing sun upon my face, and the warm breezes gently caress my bald head. For the first time, I heard the nuances in my father's laughter while he bantered with my mother. I looked at my parents and realized, at that moment, just how grateful I was for all they had done for me. My heart overflowed with love. I got it! I got what being present is! I wasn't worried about whether I would live or die or the outcomes of my upcoming treatments. I was just present to where I was and who I was with at that time. Nothing else mattered, except for *that* exact moment!

I applied my learning to everyday tasks, such as walking my dog. I slowed down, listened to the sound of the wind rustling through the trees, and curiously wondered what my dog thought as she scouted out all the scents along the way. By engaging my senses fully, I honed my ability to be present. Being present fostered gratitude, and gratitude, in turn, helped me to be present. It was a lovely self-fulfilling system.

I began to look at the opportunity of every situation. Asking myself, *"Where is the opportunity here?"* During that time, I couldn't do the things I loved to do, like dancing and traveling. However, I could still revel in the comfort that relaxing in my bed would provide. For somebody who was always on the run, being forced to be still and learn to rest was a novelty. Going to the doctor's office three times a week was certainly not fun, but I began to appreciate that I had access to top-notch healthcare. There was positivity and opportunity on every corner if I just looked for it.

I learned that being grounded in the NOW moment was the gateway to peace and gratitude. Gratitude also unfolded many gifts since each moment had the possibility of being a gift in itself. By shifting away from dwelling on past mistakes and worrying about future "what ifs," I was able to release doubt, guilt, regret, and anxiety, which granted my body the space, it needed to heal. And *that* was the ultimate gift.

Where Do I Go from Here?

It was nearly a year after initially hearing about my diagnosis. I had completed three months of chemotherapy and an eight-hour surgery, which included a double mastectomy and reconstructive surgery. A week later, I celebrated when the doctor reported that the removed breast tissue biopsy revealed that the tumor had disappeared and chemotherapy worked! The best possible scenario happened! This news meant that any cancer that might have been left behind was likely dead. I let out a sigh of relief. This long, challenging journey had paid off favorably.

So there I was…I had made it! But…wait…*Where was I exactly? What was this new ground I found myself standing upon?* Months later, after healing from surgery, life resumed back to normal. However, life felt anything *but* normal. Everything was different. I soon realized that what was different was ME. I was different. My perspective in life completely shifted. Previously, my life ran on autopilot, and now I found myself asking why I did the things I was doing. I even questioned small stuff like my hair. *Why did I have long hair my whole life? Why was I afraid to dye it red? Why did I care? If cancer didn't kill me, why did any of this matter?*

Doing the things I used to love doing felt like trying to fit a square peg into a round hole. *Who am I? What was my purpose in life?* I was standing in limbo between my old life and my new life. I had no idea how to build a bridge between them. All I knew was that I had been given a second chance at living and, this time around, I wanted to create the life that I *really* wanted. I knew I wanted my life to have purpose. I just wasn't sure what to do or how to get there.

Open to what my life could be, I was willing to explore. However, I was overwhelmed by the possibilities. Confronted by all the choices, I enlisted the help of a professional life coach. In the space that coaching provided, I connected deeply with myself. I had the opportunity to assess old beliefs and build upon those that served me while disengaging from those that did not. I got clear on what really mattered to me and identified my true passions. I consciously rebuilt my life piece by piece with intentionality. Through this process, my true identity was revealed, and it was one I had boldly chosen.

Having clarity of mind was vital for me to reintegrate back into life and reclaim my power. My self-discoveries were so potent that I committed to giving that gift back to others. I realized the best way for me to do that was to become a Certified Professional Life Coach. Coaching fulfilled the purpose I was seeking in life. Waking up every day knowing I would get to help others on their journey by empowering them to live fulfilled lives fueled me.

Cancer was a necessary interruption in my life. Because it turned my world upside down, it gave me the unique opportunity to see things from a completely different perspective. It was one I may not have gotten otherwise. I went mining for gold, seeking the lessons and opportunities that were deep within my journey. This was my pilgrimage. I came out of the other side stronger, more connected with myself, and living an intentional life full of purpose and joy.

I now get to work with others who are struggling to find what is missing in their lives by supporting them with my *Mining* methodology, so they can design the life they *really* want, achieve their goals, and live in alignment with their values. You don't have to experience a life-threatening illness or wait for a second chance in life to learn this. I believe I was meant to discover these lessons so that I could share them with you.

Below is a recap of the gold that I unearthed during my experience. I hope this inspires you to mine for the gold in your own life. Continue reading after the author biography to learn how to get my three simple strategies to shift your story and live an empowered life.

Golden Nuggets *(Lessons to Live By)*

1. **Cultivate Your Power:**

    - Choices can be challenging. Put them in perspective. Most choices are not life or death. There is no such thing as the "right" choice. Look inward to find your answers and choose the option that resonates most and serves you best, given the information you have at that moment.

    - Allow yourself the space to process your emotions. Find the courage to be authentic and vulnerable and ask for support. There is power in asking for help. Be open to what shows up, as you may get exactly what is needed, plus more.

2. **Surrender to the Present Moment:**

    - Release past regrets and anxiety around future events. Engage your senses fully and ground yourself in the present moment; see what is in front of you right now.

    - Create a positive mindset by seeking what is "right" in life. Practice gratitude daily by asking, *"What am I thankful for today? or What went right today?"*

3. **Reveal Your True Identity:**

    - Stay curious and be willing to explore all of life's possibilities.

    - Investigate limiting beliefs and create new empowering principles.

    - Identify underlying values and passions, so you can align your actions to create the life you *really* want and live life on your own terms.

Lauren Bergiel

Lauren Bergiel is a Certified Professional Life Coach who is passionate about supporting and guiding people to design the life they really want, achieve their goals, and live in alignment with their values.

With a bachelor's degree in finance, Lauren worked her way up the corporate ladder. Within five years, she became one of her company's youngest Assistant Controllers. However, she found that the corporate structure didn't afford her the flexibility she truly desired. Therefore, in 2009, she took a bold leap and left that company to start her own business.

Amid a countrywide economic crisis, Lauren faced many struggles and quickly adapted, forging a new path as a Realtor and closing over $40 million in real estate sales. She achieved everything she thought she wanted. However, something was still missing.

Then at 33, tragedy struck: Lauren was diagnosed with breast cancer. Facing a battle for her life, she trained her mind to look for opportunities and "mine for the gold" that the journey would provide. She learned to cultivate her power, surrender to the present moment, and intentionally create her identity. This is what was missing from her life and led to the fulfillment she was seeking!

Now healthy and thriving, Lauren continues to apply those lessons and is committed to sharing them with the world. She helps people connect deeply with themselves, challenge limiting beliefs, and create a roadmap that leads them to the life they *really* want.

With over 1500 hours invested in leadership, communication, and coach training, Lauren is a graduate of the Institute for Professional Excellence in Coaching (iPEC) and Landmark Worldwide and is an International Coaching Federation credentialed Associate Certified Coach.

Lauren Bergiel

Live By Lauren

Certified Professional Life Coach, ACC, ELI-MP

Lauren@LiveByLauren.com

www.LiveByLauren.com

www.Facebook.com/LiveByLauren

www.Instagram.com/Live_By_Lauren

www.LinkedIn.com/in/LaurenBergiel

3 Simple Strategies to Shift your Story and Live an Empowered Life

Download your free guide to learn how to shift your story into an empowering context and turn any circumstance or hardship into a gift or opportunity. Scan the QR code to the right or visit the website below to grab your free guide now.

www.LiveByLauren.com/m4g

Jillian Von Ohlen

From Bodybuilding to Dream Building...

As I stepped on the stage for my first bodybuilding competition, all I knew was that I wanted to win. A plethora of emotions swirling around my body was almost too much to endure, but I had made it here. I felt proud and accomplished for the hard and arduous work I did to get to this place. All the emotions were not going to hinder me, no matter what I was feeling. Thoughts of negativity then began to emerge. All the women looked better than me. They all had experience and knowledge, something I felt I lacked. I took a deep breath and told myself, "I can win! I can win! I can win!"

It all started with joining a local gym fifteen weeks earlier. There were healthy, shapely, and motivated people wherever I looked. Yes, this was the perfect place for my new endeavor of looking the part of a fitness company owner. I understood I needed a great trainer. It had to be someone who would not take any of my excuses and who would hold me accountable to what I said I wanted to achieve. I was told to see Tammie. I excitedly approached her and told her my goals and what I wanted to get out of working with her. I had recently started a dance aerobic business and wanted to take that business to the next level by creating and marketing a workout DVD and plan. I also told her that I had done personal development seminars and events for many years and that I wanted to incorporate that methodology into the DVD and fitness plan for the average woman. I understood that I needed to experience the distinction of meeting and achieving a goal, compared to simply hard work. There was a mindset that I wanted to be expressed inside of the context of this unique workout I created.

Tammie seemed to really understand my goals and aspirations. Her knowledge and years of experience were evident, and it is exactly what I knew would work for my company and me. Tammie was on many front covers of bodybuilding magazines, a competitor and winner in her own right, and a proponent of mindset and personal development. Yes, she was the one for me.

We immediately laid out a plan of action, something that all good coaches will do. I was not only impressed by her fortitude but by her commitment to me and my goals. She created a food plan, a workout plan, and weekly and monthly goals. These goals were a stretch yet reachable, which would allow me to have breakthrough results.

We trained two days per week. Within the first couple of weeks, she saw I was doing very well and sticking to the plan she created for me. At some point in those first few weeks, she mentioned in conversation how she was training a few other people to do a bodybuilding competition. I asked her if this were something I could do as well. She said yes, yet it would take a lot of work and dedication over the next 13 weeks.

The first few weeks were the most challenging. I was pushing my body to do things it had never done before. My abs hurt, my arms hurt, my legs hurt, everything hurt. Yet, I kept following the plan that Tammie created for me. There were moments, though, that I did not believe in myself and couldn't get to my end goal. What I did not realize was underneath, the results were being created. I just couldn't see it on the outside just yet. I kept pushing and giving it 100%, yet because I couldn't see it with my eyes, I didn't believe it was happening, and I felt unaccomplished. However, when you are giving 100%, regardless of the result, that is an accomplishment. Goals are to be used as a guideline, a road map, of how far you can push yourself. The intention is not to put yourself in a place of discouragement but to guide you along the way. I didn't see it as fast as I wanted. So, I kept on going and pushed through those few weeks, regardless of any negative thoughts I might have had. By the end of my second month, I was in a nice groove physically and mentally and started seeing tremendous results. It started to become second nature to wake up every day, go for a walk or run, come back home, and prep my food for the day. I would then head off to the gym to lift weights and do some more cardio. I would shower at the gym and head off to work from there. It started my day with positive thinking, motivation, and tons of energy and vitality. Every day, I felt like I could take on the world.

Tammie's due diligence and her commitment to coaching kept me on track. She stayed by my side, praising and encouraging me at every turn. There were times when I'd be lifting weights, and I'd get completely exhausted and stopped and want to quit. She would tell me, "You've got this…push through… just a few more." I can still hear her in my head today after all of these years.

As the competition got closer, Tammie changed things up a bit with both my diet and exercise regimen. I trusted her, and everything she told me to do would be the path to achieving my results. She always had my best interests in mind. We began practicing walking on stage, the positions I would have needed to do in front of the judges, and being prepared overall for what the expectations would be at the competition. I remember thinking that I felt like a science project watching how my body completely transformed. It was pretty incredible to see this amazing transformation in my health, body, and mind in such a short period of time. The results were astounding. I weighed 112 pounds and lost over 20 inches and half of my body fat.

The day of the competition finally arrived. I was as prepared as I would ever be, ready to take the stage, regardless of me being extremely nervous. As I walked onto the stage, I took a deep breath to try to calm myself while I performed my poses for the judges. Feeling a little easier, the feeling of nervousness disappeared. It left me with the ultimate feeling of being proud and accomplished. I did it! With everything I had to do to get to this exact moment, I had made it. The rigorous workouts, eating an extremely specific diet, and following my trainer's plan, was all worth it. I had never put myself through anything like this before, and I made it to the end. I was on stage a completely transformed woman, inside and out. I now knew I could achieve anything I put my mind to, knowing, after fifteen weeks of doing, the most challenging thing I had ever done was behind me. My vision became a reality. My goals were met. My plan was executed. My mindset had shifted from "Is it possible?" to "Everything is possible!" This incredible journey ended in 2011 when I chose to become a real estate agent and start a new business and raise a family.

I found myself on a new path. This path was distinctly different than the prior one with my workout video, yet unbeknownst to me at that time, it would be more similar than I could have known. This journey to becoming a real estate agent began with a desire to earn money. It wasn't a pre-set goal or an idea that was pondered. It was presented to me as a solution, and I took it not knowing how it would change my life in every way.

Real estate is not typically a career you hear much about in high school or even college. It is certainly not something you wake up and say, "Hey! I think I'm going to become a real estate agent when I grow up." So, it never really crossed my mind in the early years. In my mid-20s, I started learning more about real estate investing, which created a spark to want to discover more. I would read about people, such as Robert Kiyosaki, Donald Trump, and Warren Buffet. I would marvel at what they created. I knew I was someone who would be successful at something in my life. I just was not sure what it would be. I have come to see that real estate is a career that is so much bigger than what most people see it as. I initially saw it as an opportunity to create my own income and my own schedule. I could have it be as big as I wanted it to be, but just for me. I did not see it as an actual business of building a team or having a leveraged income. I now see real estate as an avenue to eventually be able to retire and still have "passive income" that continues without my having to be the sole person earning it. I initially saw real estate as a career created by my own efforts rather than a career that included a team with everyone's efforts.

From the get-go in 2011, after passing my test, I jumped into this career headfirst, even though I had no idea what to do or how I was going to get started. Coming from the mindset of being a real estate investor just a short time prior to this venture, I imagined what it would be like to be a successful real estate agent. There were no limits to what I could create with this new business. I was going to be coached and trained by anyone with knowledge that was willing to assist me. My intent was to soak up all the information I could get and do it quickly. I had all kinds of ideas and imagined what it would be like, especially since I had been an investor and worked on that side of the industry. However, I really didn't know anything of what I was about to embark on as a real estate agent.

I joined a smaller local brokerage and took any class that they offered. I started reading books, watching YouTube videos, and signing up for webinars. You name it. I did it. *As a side note, which I feel is important to this story, after passing my class exam, I found out I was pregnant with my first child.* What is interesting is one of the reasons I chose to do real estate was because I knew at some point in the near future, I wanted to start a family and wanted flexibility with my schedule. I just had no idea I would be starting a family that soon.

During my first six months in real estate, while pregnant, I sold two homes and did about half a dozen rentals. Keep in mind; this was in 2011 when the market was at the bottom from the crash. Thus, I barely made any money. In 2012, I gave birth to our son in January and closed fifteen homes working only ten months that year, and now raising a newborn. I quickly discovered the type of schedule that worked for my new business and new baby.

In 2013, I hired my first part-time assistant and made triple of what I did in 2012, and ranked in the top five single agents in my office. That same year in September, my husband joined my team. The business was flourishing, and I could not handle all the new leads and referrals on my own. There were just not enough hours in the day to take care of them properly, and I prided myself on customer service. Therefore, this was the most lucrative and satisfying solution. It brought more money into our home, which allowed me to have my assistant work longer hours. This also took some of the burdens off my shoulders. We were a duo and all our clients loved it! I realized that building a team was better in every way, so I began that path to exploring how I would accomplish that.

Shortly after him joining me and quitting his 20-year career in grocery retail, I hired my first sales coach to allow me to achieve even bigger goals. During this time, I realized I needed an operational system, transaction system, and marketing system. I couldn't find much of anything on the market, so I worked on creating my own systems and processes. I put together checklists, spreadsheets, pre-written emails, scripts, presentations, creative marketing, etc. I was obtaining leads in various ways, including organic "Gorilla" leads through marketing on Craigslist and through my Zillow profile, as well as paid leads through a variety of sources. It was fun and enjoyable to create these systems, put them into action and see them working for me.

During the beginning stages, most of my success was from pure motivation and focus while learning what the "big dogs" in the industry were doing. I simply copied and pasted. There were many times, though, I took one step forward and two steps back. I never fully understood the saying, "The more you fall, the more you learn," until becoming a real estate business owner. I fell down a lot and got back up every time, having learned something new. I remembered my personal development coach saying, "Breakdowns create breakthroughs." Hiring a great coach, setting up a roadmap and a focused plan, and doing my own personal development was what it took to get me to the next level and have breakthrough results, not only for my business, but it also trickled into my personal and family life.

That same year, my current brokerage closed, and after extensive research, I moved to be with a large, national company that was known for its training, culture, and growth. I immediately stepped into their Agent Leadership Council, where I was a part of making decisions for the office to run more efficiently. I quickly became one of their instructors, teaching classes to new agents on how to get started in this business and do it effectively. I became one of the "go-to" agents in the office, supporting other agents with their vision and plan for their business.

By 2014, I was ranked in the top 3% nationwide, closing 50+ deals that year. After creating my own systems, hiring a coach, and implementing my game plan, I was able to achieve much more than I ever anticipated. I clearly understood that it is much more difficult to reach your goals on your own. This realization began with my bodybuilding project and continued and grew throughout the years in real estate.

As the years progressed, I continued to teach, train and support agents at all different levels. This included both new and seasoned agents. I continued to grow my team and rank in the top five teams in my office. We were ranked in the top 1% locally and continued to stay at the top 3% nationwide. I eventually copywrote the system I created and started selling it to agents in my office and within my local area. The agents that used my manual, "The Prosperous Agent System," and put the technology into action achieved amazing results. This assisted these agents in meeting their expectations in every way. It made me feel that my hard work and love for this industry was finally recognized. Some agents shared that they had a 30% increase in revenue from simply adding my system to what they were already doing. Seeing the success, it was creating in my local market and already enjoying coaching and training agents in my office sparked a fire within me to want to share my system, training, and coaching with other agents across the country. I started doing some research on the statistics of what agents succeed and fail in this business. I was astounded at the results. The numbers showed that only 13% of agents sell more than 12 homes per year, and the top 3% of that 13% sell more than 30 homes per year. I couldn't accept that. I knew that I could make a difference and impact agents by supporting them in achieving whatever they wanted to create in their business and their life. I saw many gaps and areas that were missing that could be improved. It was an opportunity for me to support agents in a bigger way than had ever been done before. *This was a defining moment where I realized I wanted to be a real estate coach.* I knew that I could transform the industry and create something that was not really being done. I was committed to not allow these agents to fail. The more research I did, the more astounded I was with what I found. There are coaches in the industry that have not actually sold real estate or who use old ways to generate leads that no longer work. They also don't hold you accountable or create a plan tailored for you that will actually work. I could go on and on. I could not accept where the industry was and what was being tolerated. I felt a strong desire to do something about it. For that reason, I took that desire and passion and started my real estate coaching business.

I understood that hiring a great coach would not only enhance my business but also have it reach new heights in a much shorter period of time. After researching different coaches, their core values, and their methodology, I found the perfect person to assist me in my new business venture. As I moved forward with this newly created vision to transform the real estate industry, I realized that the challenges to be met were more than I could do to its completion. The challenge of combining coaching and selling real estate was not working for me. I initially thought I could combine the two, yet it was clear they were two separate businesses. I desperately wanted to coach agents, yet I was not able to make it work with the real estate team I was building and growing. Something was going to suffer, and my current team and sales were already suffering. I could not allow that to happen, so I needed to make a decision.

During this realization, I was coaching with a top agent. He shared an opportunity with me to become one of his business partners. I saw a way that I could continue building and growing my real estate business while coaching agents at the same time without either of them suffering. This epiphany was huge for me, as I was being given an opportunity to do both. My goals shifted into a new realm. It was an arena where I could meet the demands of real estate as an agent and leader for my team, as well as excel in my new business as a coach. My mindset moved into a new dimension, knowing that I created this opportunity. I put in the hard work, executed the plan. It was all paying off. This new place was not only incredibly experiential and exciting but a place I knew I could make a huge difference in people's businesses and lives.

Coaching agents has the same foundation and mindset, and principles as to what I learned prior with my bodybuilding business. These principles encompass creating a vision, hiring a coach to hold you accountable and creating a solid plan, putting it into action to reach your goals, and seeing it all come to fruition. This has held true for me for many years, and I repeatedly see it become a reality for agents I get to coach.

After ten amazing years in the real estate business, I have discovered many things that this industry has to offer. Many of these opportunities I never knew were possible. I continue to be a student of the industry as I develop and grow personally and professionally. As the saying goes, *"The best teacher is first a great student."* That statement could not be truer when it comes to being successful in anything you set out to accomplish in your life. Learn and grow as much as you can, establish a vision, create and follow the right system and plan, and watch where life will take you. I have, and the ride has been so incredible.

Jillian Von Ohlen

Jillian Von Ohlen is a real estate broker associate, mompreneur, trainer, coach, author, and founder of The Prosperous Agent System and Mompreneurs Unleashed. Jillian is recognized as a leader in the real estate industry by ranking in the top 3% nationwide and the top 1% in her local market. Jillian has been featured in Top Agent Magazine and The Expert Network. For over 30 years, Jillian's key to success has been mastering personal development, which is an ongoing life practice. Jillian transforms people's perception to master their highest self in relation to their business, relationships, and life. Her constant learning is passed on to her coaching clients. Jillian attributes her success to the systems she has set in place to streamline her processes, as well as the various coaches she has hired along the way to support her and hold her accountable. Jillian's focus and stick-to-it attitude helps her keep going every day. "In business, you are either surviving or thriving, and your mindset and support system makes all the difference." Jillian specializes in leadership, motivation, and sales training. She is passionate and committed to having those around her realize their full potential. She empowers and inspires people to live a life of joy, freedom, and ease. When Jillian is not helping Realtors achieve their highest levels of performance, she enjoys spending time with her family and friends in Port St Lucie, FL. She enjoys reading books about customer service, selling, marketing, and branding, personal growth, and the human performance. She also enjoys healthy eating and exercising, live music, and vacationing with her family and friends. Her deepest passion and life goal is to help end human trafficking and support trafficked survivors.

Jillian Von Ohlen
772-214-8530
Jillian@VonOhlenTeam.com
www.JillianVonOhlen.com
www.Instagram.com/Jillian.VonOhlen

5 Easy Steps to Get More Listings and Close More Deals

Every real estate agent knows the value of obtaining and closing seller leads. Jillian's step-by-step guide and video series show you exactly how to get more listings and close more deals, regardless of the real estate market.

What's Included:

- Swipe Ad Copy to Ensure Sellers Hear Your Message
- Proven Resources to Save You Time & Money
- Follow-up Strategies That Will Get You Results!

Grab your FREE guide and video series NOW!

Use Code OMFREE ($29 Value)

www.ListingsMiniCourse.com

Lindsey Oaks

Dreams Carried on Horseback

Horse Crazy

I believe that I was born with a love of horses coursing through my veins, wanting to ride horses from my earliest memories. Had my father known what he was getting himself into when he drove me to my first horseback riding lesson, I feel sure he would have turned the car around and headed in the other direction. In fact, he had me try every sport in existence before allowing me to settle on horses. Not that he had a choice; unique talent is required to strike out in T-ball.

My reputation in town as the "horse girl" solidified when I began to show up to classes in high school smelling of dirt and sweat after getting up early to care for and train my horse before school. Therefore, it should have come as no surprise when I announced that upon graduation, I would be moving to Kentucky, the horse capital of the world, to pursue riding as a profession.

Oversized Dreams

I don't come from a very wealthy family, so I hadn't spent years competing at nationally rated events like some of my peers. Paying for high-quality horses, training, and competitions were out of the question for us. To make it to the pro levels, I would have to find a "working student" position to acquire the experience that I needed. Working students make the world go round in the competition horse world. Toiling away for free or extraordinarily little pay, working students are a cheap alternative to paying actual professionals to care for these equine athletes. They put in long hours and demanding physical work in return for knowledge, experience, and the chance to stand out against hundreds of other kids vying for the few well-paying jobs in the industry. I was no different.

Luckily, in my ignorance, I landed in a place where I could get a real taste for what it would be like to ride at the top. I spent my first year in Kentucky at Team CEO Eventing, working alongside several other girls with the same big dreams. The program was instrumental in giving me a leg up on the years of competition I had missed. That first summer, I was allowed to compete several times a month on multiple horses. The time spent in the competition ring made up for the long hours falls off young horses and budget that only allowed for eating and sleeping. I loved every minute.

I knew that to really "make it" as a trainer, I would need something to establish my authority. It would have to be something I could point to that would say, "This is proof that I know what I'm doing, and you should pay me to do it for you." I knew just the thing.

In my chosen sport of "eventing," the holy grail of competition is the "Rolex Kentucky Three-Day Event" (now with the name Landrover Kentucky Three-Day). A grueling test of horse and rider spread out over three days; the competition begins with the "dressage" test, a prescribed sequence of movements that the pair must execute with grace and precision. On the second day of competition, crowds of up to 33,000 pack into the Kentucky Horse Park to watch the horses and riders head into the countryside, galloping over four miles of taxing terrain at speeds of up to 25 miles per hour. The pair must jump into and out of water obstacles, over ditches, and over jumps up to four feet tall! On the third day, after all of that, the horse must come back fresh to jump over a course of obstacles called "show jumps" in a large stadium arena, showing that he and his rider have the mental and physical fitness to continue after the most challenging work of their lives. This "horse triathlon" is the only one of its kind in the northern hemisphere and one of only four in the world. I knew I had to do it.

Luckily for me, the trainer for whom I worked had a talented yet dangerously quirky horse for sale that I had been training as part of my work. "Taylor" was athletic, unpredictable, and so aggressive when heading to a jump that I'd sometimes lose control of him. It was a combination of traits that often left me on the ground, spitting dirt. I knew he was just crazy enough to take me around Rolex, so long as I could hang on long enough to get to the finish line. After pitching my master plan to anyone and everyone who would listen, I managed to sell my parents, David and Anne Oaks, and my godfather Robbie Faircloth on the idea. We scraped up enough money to buy him between the four of us, and just like that, all our dreams hinged on Taylor.

Building Our Tribe

The first few years with Taylor, although challenging, were rewarding. My inability to rein in his exuberance while jumping seemed to my coaches to prove that I was training him to do his job with confidence. However, as we climbed the levels of competition into the international ranks, the cracks began to show. We still hadn't mastered any "grace and precision" for our dressage tests, the first competition phase. He had little interest in working as a team, and at five foot four inches and barely over one hundred pounds, there was little that I could do to make him.

In addition to Taylor and my communication issues, I was dead broke. Working in the horse business, I was often able to trade work for Taylor's board, food, and sometimes even a ride to a competition. However, that still left vet bills, farrier bills, equipment bills, and competition entries to be paid. I survived on ramen noodles and coffee and worked multiple jobs at any given time.

It was during these years that I learned the power of developing my tribe. The "horsey" network that I built frequently bailed me out of trouble. When I'd have to quit a job to go to a week-long competition, a friend would land me a position to return to. When I couldn't afford board for Taylor, a friend would recommend a farm where I could keep him in return for riding a few horses for the owner.

I was looking for a new farm to house Taylor, when a friend in my network told me about a new trainer in town. Eric Dierks had competed at Rolex himself and knew the path to the top. I knew that I desperately needed help, so I called him right away to start training.

For the first time in our career, someone else set Taylor's work schedule for the week. Eric pushed me to ride aggressively to the jumps, even when Taylor pulled me to go faster. He explained that Taylor felt trapped and that asking him to go slower and slower made him fight me more. I had to compromise and give a little to get a little.

In addition to our newfound compromises on control, I added two new members to my support team in the year that followed.

Drew Kemerling became "Taylor's slave," taking over most of his care and spoiling him like the professional athlete he was. Having her there to help manage him and the other parts of my horse business allowed me to focus more on myself and what I needed to be successful.

The second addition was a family friend, Bill Edwards, who had invested in a few horses with me over the years. He bought into Taylor as another owner, giving my finances some much-needed breathing room.

All of this fell into place to create Taylor's best year on record. Our partnership was now six years old, and we would make our first real splash in upper-level eventing. We moved to the level just below our goal event that year, earning ribbons each time we entered an international level competition. We finished the year in the top ten at the Fair Hill International Three–Day Event, a final steppingstone and qualifier for Rolex.

After six years of driving around the country competing, sacrificing holidays to work for Taylor's dinner, and saving money on hotel fees by sleeping in my truck at big events, we had made it! We were on our way to the Rolex Kentucky Three–Day Event!

Dead Dreams

It was a chilly but otherwise lovely day in April 2013, when Taylor and I trotted into the arena to make our debut at the Rolex. My hands were shaking as I halted to salute the judge and begin my dressage test, the first test of the competition. The dressage test is a test of harmony, balance, and grace. Dressage is often described as a ballet on horseback, but the packed stadium made it difficult to be graceful. The footsteps, whispers, and movements of a couple of thousand people made the atmosphere electric. We were both tense. Taylor leaned toward explosive instead of calm and collected. The test was sub-par, but I was proud, nonetheless. Who knew that some kid from South Georgia with only determination could make it to the world stage?

The next day was the cross country test. I knew Taylor was fit enough to gallop the four miles required and brave enough to jump all the jumps. I knew this would be his time to shine! Thirty thousand people lined the gallop lanes, which are the ropes holding back spectators so that the horses could gallop their course unimpeded. The moment we left the starting box, I knew I was in trouble. The crowds were large, the announcer was loud, and Taylor was suddenly a dragon underneath me.

I rode conservatively, trying to regain control of the speed and direction. It was no use. As the minutes ticked by, I developed painful cramps in my sides from struggling to hold him back. We racked up penalties all over the course after a particularly hairy moment galloping down a hill towards a substantial four-foot obstacle while entirely out of control. I pulled up and retired from the competition. I could no longer feel my fingers, and my strength was giving out. Taylor pranced back to the barns as if he hadn't just been galloping for nine solid minutes. Just like that, my dream was dead.

We didn't do much competing for the rest of the year. I was devastated, and my bank account was empty. I was behind on all my bills. After the scariest ride of my life, I didn't feel the need to try to regroup. I put Taylor up for sale. I needed the money, and I had promised Taylor's owners that one day they'd see a return on their investment for years, so I figured now would be as good a time as any.

Failing Forward

That fall, I took a seasonal job in Arkansas, planning to return to Kentucky in the spring. There was little to no interest in a horse that had gone nuts on the world stage, so Taylor came with me.

We spent our days playing. We rode through the mountains and jumped over logs in our path. Out in the woods, far away from the hustle of competitions and the day-to-day training, something changed. Taylor and I just enjoyed each other. I forgave him for being who he had always been. I told him I was sorry for the pressure I had put on him to change.

Since his last competition on record was our terrible run at Rolex, I knew selling him would be rather tricky. Therefore, I decided to take him down to Texas a couple of times to compete over the winter. It was nothing exciting, just some low-level competition to get him sold and move on.

The break had done us both some real good. We came out blazing, picking up ribbons at our first competition in nine months. "It's crazy," I remember telling my mother, "but we are still qualified for Rolex next year. We need only one competition at that level to knock the dust off, and we could do it!"

I drove back to Texas again that February, having entered Taylor in his first advanced level competition since Rolex. I had every confidence that we'd pick up as if we hadn't left off. Then I promptly fell off of him at the third jump on course. So much for knocking the dust off.

"I'm fine!" I told my mom on the phone, "All I have to do is drive through the night to an advanced competition in Virginia, knock the dust off there instead, and then we could do it!" I asked her to loan me a couple of hundred bucks to get me there. We then drove through the night to Virginia, where I slept in my truck like the old days. Taylor was a little less wild than he had been the previous weekend. We didn't get a ribbon, but we did what we needed to do. We were back.

So, on the way back to Kentucky, I called my mom to ask for one more loan. I needed one hundred dollars to enter the Rolex Kentucky Three-Day Event one more time.

Back From the Grave

This time I was calm, trotting into the stadium for our dressage test. Although my dream had risen from the dead, I had nothing to lose at this point. Pretty much everyone I knew thought I had lost my mind. To have such a terrible result the first time around, prove absolutely nothing all year, and come back again was plain stupid. However, I knew that Taylor had the training needed to make it happen. He had been surprised by the noisy crowds, and I hadn't known how to help him. This time, I had a plan.

I willed my body to stay relaxed. I reminded myself that I couldn't do any worse than I had the year before. Although still exuberant at times when he shouldn't have been, we beat our previous year's score on the dressage test by five whole points! Everyone noticed the change, and I was interviewed by the press several times that day.

Day Two, the cross-country test loomed. The weather was inconsistent. I worried that I'd have to try to control Taylor in the rain, trying to hold onto slippery reins. As our time came, the rain, thankfully, held off. I had some new equipment, designed to help me hold onto Taylor without expending all my energy in the process and a new plan. LET HIM GO. I tried to remember Eric's teachings. Give a little to get a little. It takes two to fight. I wouldn't try to hold him back this time. If he wanted to run, I'd let him. I couldn't afford to fight with him for the next four miles.

We left the start box and jumped the first obstacle. As planned, I relaxed my grip on the reins. Taylor was gone. The next few jumps were a speeding blur, but so far, I could interject my opinion just enough before each jump to keep us from going totally off course. However, at the first water obstacle, a jump down into the water, followed by a ninety-degree right turn to a massive jump out of the water, I found out a little too late that I had given Taylor too much room to run. I couldn't make the turn. Instead, Taylor ran for the spectators, jumping the little rope designed to separate us. Now, in the middle of a crowd of people, I tried not to panic. Thankfully, we hadn't run anyone over, and the crowd had quickly given us space. Incredibly, the jump judge maintained the crowd's order, let down the rope, and allowed us to continue quickly.

As we galloped through the rest of the course, Taylor began to settle, and I was able to slow him to a respectable speed. He ate up the rest of the course, and we were able to gallop through the finish flags into a second crowd of people — our tribe of owners and supporters were all waiting at the finish for us.

On the third day, Taylor showed up enthusiastic as ever, as if he hadn't galloped four miles and jumped 35 obstacles in twelve minutes the day before. We jumped the stadium course before a crowd of 6,000 people. Taylor had brought our dreams back from the grave, finishing in 35th place out of 60 starters from all over the globe!

Educated in the Saddle

These days, I continue to work in the equestrian world, leveraging my experience at Rolex to position me as a top player in the game. I've also expanded my business to help coaches, online entrepreneurs, influencers, and speakers develop and project their personal brands in the online space. The lessons that I have learned on my journey to the top allow me to develop strategies to help my clients' deliver their messages to the world, increase lead generation and ultimately sales.

Here are a few of the lessons I learned from Taylor that I use to help my clients in their journey to becoming visible.

Show It Who's Boss

You've heard somewhere that when handling a horse, you have to "show it who's boss." That idea is a little aggressive for reality, but the idea rings true. When working with horses, especially a quirky horse like Taylor, you must be very clear with the horse on where you stand in the relationship and what you want from him. Horses have stringent rules about structure within groups or herds as a group of horses is called. In a herd, every horse is either above or below you in the pecking order. No two horses sit in the same place in the hierarchy. From a horse's point of view, a person who walks into his stall and tells him what to do, but doesn't walk with a straight back and has darting eyes that say, "I'm not very sure that you will do what I tell you," is very confusing. In life and business, a leader must send out a message that is consistent on all fronts. When you speak words that don't align with your actions, you confuse people. This will get you the same effect with people as it does with a horse: negative results.

Point to the Proof That You Know Your Stuff

I did this in the equestrian world by completing one of the toughest competitions in the world. It's on my resume forever. I'm doing it for myself as a consultant by writing in this book, speaking on podcasts as an expert, and creating courses for others who want to learn.

What accomplishments can you use to position yourself as the "go-to" person in your field of expertise? Don't stop at one thing. Speak on that podcast, accept that invitation to write a guest blog, and let the world know about your unique talents and skills! These are ways to stand out against the competition to make an impact!

It Takes Years to Become an Overnight Success

The journey to breaking into the big leagues can be long and tiring. Many people won't make it because they quit too soon.

Because a horse is a prey animal, it sees a human trying to get onto his back, like a tiger trying to eat him. Running fast and bucking hard is a defense against tigers. So, in the beginning, I wasn't fixated on making it to Rolex. I just worked on letting Taylor get used to me getting on and off of his back. Then he learned to carry me around. Months later, we walked over a pole on the ground. Eventually, that pole turned into a jump that we'd confidently gallop over.

Break down big goals into bite-sized steps. Be ready to invest in the long term and learn to celebrate small wins on your way to the top. Real success takes time to produce. It doesn't happen overnight!

I had no idea that over our seven-year journey to the top, Taylor was preparing me to be a leader and teaching me the value of investing in the long-term. The lessons he taught me have become a framework for me to assist others on their journey. I am indebted to him for every sliver of wisdom.

Lindsey Oaks

At the tender age of 17, Lindsey Oaks informed her parents that she would be moving 500 miles away to pursue a career competing horses as a professional upon graduation from school. She did this even though she'd never competed in a regulation competition! Over the next decade, Lindsey would repeatedly learn how to become an entrepreneur the hard way. She did make it, establishing herself as a competitor on the world stage and as a top-tier horse trainer and coach to aspiring equestrians. During a stint working in the racehorse industry, Lindsey convinced her boss to buy her an "expensive camera" to provide owners of young racehorses with nice photographs of their future stars in training. She quickly found, however, that she had no idea how to work this fancy equipment! A crash course in photography, and a few years later, Lindsey launched a photography business creating branding images specifically for entrepreneurs. Right away, Lindsey saw that many of the starving artists, creative freelancers, and brilliant speakers hiring her, had no idea how to seize their own personal brand's marketing power. Realizing that her unique experience as a coach provided her with the opportunity to help others reach their potential, she began assisting them in developing clear, cohesive messaging across platforms.

Lindsey now lives in the Chicago suburbs with her favorite model: her dog Leroy. She spends her time teaching "horse-crazy kids" (and adults) to communicate effectively with 1000 lb. animals who don't speak English and creating strategies for coaches, consultants, and influencers to communicate with the world. Her clients describe her as a coffee-addicted, high-energy smarty pants, who tells stories to teach lessons.

To learn personal branding tips like "How to: Embrace the Camera, for Camera-Shy Businesswomen" and "How to: Be Friends with Google," visit Lindsey at: www.LindseyOaks.com.

Lindsey Oaks
Lindsey Oaks Photography
1427 Wesley Court
Mundelein, IL 60060
859-457-9042
Lindsey@LindseyOaks.com
www.LindseyOaks.com

Content Creation Made Easy

Tired of posting on Facebook every day and wondering if you're doing it right? My content creation course will help you clarify who you are creating content for and what you want to accomplish with each piece of content. You will also learn content repurposing and recycling strategies. (Because we are not all content spitting machines!) You'll never wonder if you are "doing it right" again.

Get the Course for Free With This Coupon: EMPOWEREDWOMEN

www.LearnToBrandYourself.com/courses/contentcreation

Mona Aburmishan

Comedy 101: Unconditional Forgiveness

The Exciting Truth of Teaching Stand Up Comedy!
Email Answers to Mona@MonaComedy.com

*"Not everything that is faced can be changed, but nothing
can be changed until it is faced."*

—Philosopher James Baldwin

The Why: When People Feel Safe to Express Their Truth, in Play, They Have Room For…?

The Pandemic of 2020/2021 presents an exciting rose gold lining. Kids and adults have begun to express their creative side in communion. It seems that we have all started using modalities of comedy and performance videos to feel safe in expressing our passions and truths in ways we could have never imagined decades ago. Through joke-telling, sketch performances, and funny internet videos, we have inspired future generations to allow for more laughter, play, and real discovery in all areas of our lives. As a result, people become emotional when navigating media and sense the need for the truth now more than ever — ***just because your backgrounds are palm trees doesn't mean your life is!***

For society becoming fully online while learning to navigate the live video calls, meetings, and odd errands, is like a woman having to get a zoom-divorce as the judge's cat joins the session. It has us aware of how much of our behavior is observed in ways that previous generations did not face. Each video meeting will showcase layers of new information, all hiding-in-plain-sight.

There is no need to worry. We are in a whole new world, and because so, I'd like to help you feel more grounded in your own-ness! Therefore, my article is slightly different because it requires you, the reader, to engage.

Would you like to join?

If your answer is **NO**, this article will be a fun story about *HOW* a stand-up comedian has been teaching comedy to diverse communities in America, South Africa, and beyond. [PS: #TeamNo, offer this article to your favorite stranger.]

If your answers are **YES**, this article will be a fun workshop in *WHY* a stand-up comedian has been teaching comedy worldwide.

#TeamYes

This article is **your** complementary Comedy 101 Class, as my small token of gratitude to you for the personal healing you are doing publicly or privately. Thank you for taking a minute each day to center yourself before throwing a fit at someone for something that you are totally valid for wanting to throw. Thank you for choosing to be a **comedian** today and choosing to find ways of turning frustrating into funny! GRAB A PEN & PAPER. [#TeamNo, you can read this and imagine #TeamYes writing alongside you.]

Journaling Exercise 1: Begin Writing for [5 MINUTES]
"What's the Difference Between a Comedian and a Non-Comedian?"

Helpful Definitions:

Stand Up Comedy is an energetic style of communication in which a single person performs in front of a live audience. "A stand-up comic defines their craft by how they convince the audience to laugh and by their development of a persona."

*A **Bit** or **Joke*** is a non-sexual story [yes, friends, there are other subjects to talk about], an observation, or complaint set up as an engaging logical argument, premise, inference, and conclusion; with someone or something (text, family pets), in a neutral state and posed with the expectation of a response without language. There are only body movements or likes on social media. Jokes usually have two subtypes: inductive reasoning and deductive reasoning. The main difference between inductive and deductive reasoning is that inductive reasoning aims at developing a theory [i.e., Black Lives Matter Movement]. In contrast, deductive reasoning aims at testing an existing theory [i.e., examining thoroughly the state of Black Life today]. Inductive reasoning moves from specific observations [my life] to broad generalizations [our lives], and deductive reasoning the other way around.

[BONUS POINTS: How many of your favorite comics are former social workers, educators, lawyers, or doctors?]

Class Clown: A student, as applied in the positive, tries to make other students laugh. In the **negative**, one who is **a *Bully:*** A person who uses strength or power to harm or intimidate those who are weaker. ***Synonyms*** *for a bully,* persecutor, oppressor, tyrant, ruffian, thug, attack dog, badass. [Interesting ending Webster, I see you, yeesh better keep an eye on our bullies!]

The Heckler: The complainer, the distractor, annoyance in your life as in a real human, or technology that dings at the wrong times. Heckler is the real bully in the room that distracts us from focus and flow state. If not a real emergency, the Heckler is a powerful energy leak through chaos and confusion. [I.e., people who drink too much at the late show but haven't eaten are usually hecklers in any comedy club. Once drunk, suddenly they're funnier than the comic and yell at the stage to feel special.]

Post-Modern Stand-Up Comedy: An international "stage vs. audience" artform, where American and European racialized discourse no longer applies. International stand-up comedy must address each community group's multi-ethnic nuances or legacy as valid and uniquely perfect; otherwise, someone is likely to be offended. One person's "weird" is another person's "not weird at all." Therefore, in international comedy, the comedian must dig much deeper into a community's news, documentaries, and history books to better understand what conflicts happened before running their mouth about perspectives on class, race, or religion outside of their home country.

"Stand Up Comedy is America's real diplomatic agent."

It is critical that international comedians only punch up in optimism. They teach others the fun in elevating *conflict resolution* by adhering to universal codes of respectful language for audiences to resonate positively and illicit self-discovery and possibility within a safe structure. For example, American comedians performing in English-speaking territories may feel extremely offended by the word "fag." It became a colloquial term for "a cigarette" or "loose square" within the former British colonies but is heavily derogatory in the U.S. Therefore, just like you, a comedian is intentional about each word's value in the environment. It is normal to feel as if you are always intentionally self-editing, language, and material, to accommodate the change. English's linguistic structure has been changing rapidly and must be used with caution internationally. Having a keen eye for embed bias in language will help you create very clever material and keep the world laughing!

Journaling Exercise 2: [5 MINUTES]
"It is certain, in any case, that ignorance, allied with power, is the most ferocious enemy justice can have."
—Philosopher James Baldwin

How does this quote and the above definitions resonate with you?

<u>Context</u>: Finding Your Inner Bully and Asking, "U Good?"

Most comedians have asked themselves, "What is my comedy voice? Can I even write a joke? How can I be better?" "Why do I want to be a comedian?" "What style of comedy do I want to practice?" "Hey self, am I a comedian that wants fame *for* impact, or am I a comedian using fame *to* impact?"

Meaning: Am I using my voice to change the environment, or am I merely making fun of the environment to keep it the same and make *me* look cool? [Like karma, be intentional about your outward and inward dialogue, it's always present.]

Journaling Exercise 3: [5 MINUTES]
"What's one yukky childhood memory you love telling because it makes others laugh?"

Set your timer for five minutes but before you begin writing, pull out your favorite music playlist.

Chicago Style: Where Fear Is Funny, and Frustration Is Always Insightful!

Rule #1: Set your tone and think before you speak! But first, find your favorite rhythm!

Sound Check: Music has a subtle impact on all of us by being the background harmony of life. Especially as a professional stand-up comedian, it's the necessary outlier to every comedy performance. Not commonly known, we work alone but somehow can host the Oscars. Music helps us connect with our vibration, and for a comic, it gets us in a zone. As a new comic, you'll feel like most athletes preparing for an event. Music helps us to navigate our personal life, while also mentally mapping out the perfect performance for strangers. To have a great connection with the crowd, a comedian must be willing to be fully responsible for their personal energy field, aka the "VIBES" brought to the club are as important as the "VIBES" taken from the club. The crowd really does make or break a comedian's night. However, in the same vein, a comedian can make or break an audience member's date or a fun outing with their mistress. Gone are the days of the comedian bullying the lone couple upfront. You never know who you are insulting! Comedy, pre-and post-COVID, places great effort on appeasing the crowd before the comedian gets on stage. It is evident in the menu, the music, and the venue's overall ambiance. Getting there early to observe all environmental clues will help any comedian have an all-around stellar performance.

Journaling Exercise 4: [5 MINUTES]
How's your vibe right now?

Observe the ambiance of your environment. What is working vs. what is annoying you? How could background music, incense, or a change in lighting make you feel better?

As stand-up comedians, we are always in thought overdrive to find the funny. For example, when picking out a song, if you put on Tupac or Biggie, would you feel empowered or remorsefully nostalgic at their tragic end? How might that impact the whole show, if we played only these two artists throughout the night? How might the audience feel at the end of the show?

Comedians typically book their own business and keep in mind the overall impact on each audience member's experience as they head home. What is the client's "take-aways" is important for all businesses, just as it is for a working comedian or independent artist. Just like you, dealing with our finance department, the sales department, the marketing department, and any department you could imagine, while also accounting for human resources, is tiresome, annoying, and is the fun, boring part of a comic's life. As silly as this may sound, if I sexually harass myself, I will have to file a claim against myself.

Journaling Exercise 5: [5 MINUTES]
"What are the three amazing habits that you would claim to the world?"

Try replacing the word "amazing" with "smelly" and "habits"
with friends/family/uber drivers.

Closing Session: A Story's "Re-Tell" Value

Setting the Scene:

Springtime Chicago, a blonde hair blue-eyed 60+year old with her "brown" [1/2 Arab] Muslim comedian daughter standing in a packed local Chicago South-Loop Grocery Store on a Sunday. It's Lent and Passover and soon Ramadan, *so The Spirit must be around both women* since the store is packed. The pressure is, therefore, ON to get the groceries and get home to enjoy what's left of Sunday before that Monday morning work-life ensues.

The cashier is a middle-aged indigenous presenting Latina woman working as fast as possible to get the groceries to the end of the belt, where the young man with what seems like special abilities is taking his time to carefully place each item in the "right" place as he works, slightly unaware of the pressure all around him.

Similarly, feeling the environment's pressure, the comedian's daughter walks over to ask if the young man could use more help, given the size of the grocery order coming at him and the backed-up belt. She hovers and then asks to help, when he blurts, "I'M THE BAGGER!" She jolts back. Shocked, the comedian was frightened, as if she had done something wrong or offended the young man. She replied with, "OK, I'm sorry," but kept hearing "I'm the bagger" in her head over and over. Just as she had done after every show or when learning new languages, the comedian asked herself repeatedly, "Was there something I did to make him feel as if I wanted his job?" "Did he not appreciate my wanting to help?" "Did my mom really need all these damn groceries…oh, look, some chicken salad, I can't wait to eat that…no, wait, why did that guy snap off at me?" "You know if this kid shows up at a comedy club anytime soon, I'm going to roast him for snapping off at me in front of my mother. However, only if he's able-bodied and just being a jerk" "But! If he's special needs and is taking his time, as we all should, then good for him, he's doing great!"

All random discovery questions and common thoughts, running through the mind of anyone in that moment.

Once the bagger completed the work and the mother paid for the groceries, the daughter and mom walked to the car. The mom slowly looked at her daughter questioningly. This triggered the daughter again into thought-overdrive-think-mode, "Oh no, watch this, is my mom about to snap at me for somehow bullying a special abilities dude at the grocery store? Is she going to bring up the past now, just because I bullied my sisters for being slow to pick up their toys decades ago?" "Because she knows I'm always looking for great material for the stage, is she going to lecture me about how I aggravated the guy and why I didn't help him faster?" "Is my mother somehow going to think I was bullying this poor guy? Really, he kind of snapped at me, but I don't want to assume he's special needs. However, if he isn't then, I deserve a Nobel Peace Prize for not opening my comedian-Chicago-style-smart-mouth and potentially causing unnecessary harm on a Sunday by being in defense mode to his quick statement. Is she going to make fun of my Arab and or my Muslim temper as being reasons I can't leave a poor bagger guy alone at work?" Exhausted, the daughter looked up at the mother, who quietly said, "Mona, you know he WAS the bagger, right?!" Shocked and speechless, both the mom and the daughter busted out laughing.

Journaling Exercise 6: [5 MINUTES]
"Why did the mother and daughter laugh?"

Explain times your judgment of another confused you.

The Comedy Midwife: Access to our Healer Society.

Social philosopher, psychoanalyst, and activist Dr. Franz Fanon, famously postulated that the identity, **wellness**, and possible neuroses of colonial and post-colonial society are directly correlated to language. In one of his most notable works, *Black Skin, White Masks*, he states: "We attach a fundamental importance to the phenomenon of language and consequently consider the study of language essential for providing us with one element in understanding the black man's dimension of being-for-others, it being understood that to speak is to exist absolutely for the other."

A former comedy student of mine, also a physician at a local school [University of Chicago], asked me to speak on stand-up comedy and medicine. In preparation for that workshop, I was asked: ***"How could physicians benefit from learning a few skills of stand-up comedy and the mindset of a stand-up comedian? If you were to teach physicians stand-up comedy, what would you teach them and why?"***

[Feel Free to Answer This Question Yourself as Part of Your Bonus Homework #2]

Answer: All professionals that deal with the public, including humans, animals, or aliens, all could benefit from a few simple yet complex techniques in emotional intelligence that stand-up comedians use every day. Similarly, a physician's objective is to guide others to be well. Both the physician and the comedian must deal with the unknown and see all humans as equal!

The VOICE: Methods to find and cultivate your voice — so patients can really hear you and you could really hear them! Work extensively in finding effective self-expression methods, self-discovery, and gratitude through micro-expressions and body language will show others your genuine interest in being there to provide authentic care! I also invite patients to be as authentic as possible!

Physician: *"Hello Mr. Jackson, thank you for choosing to see me today; how can I best be of service!"*

Mr. Jackson: *"Thanks Doc. I'd rather not be at the doctor, honestly, but I appreciate your perspective!"*

The LISTENING: Finding and cultivating your listening ear — How quickly can a doctor pick up non-verbal cues: name origins, body language patterns, and observations from the micro and macro environment? How can instincts of the non-clinical world best serve a patient's needs? Do I have all the information I need to make the best opening statement, or might there be a pre-approved opinion about this person hidden somewhere in our cultures? More importantly, how might this patient perceive me, through their pre-approved lens, given how I look, sound, or what I'm wearing? How might their wellness be better served by knowing more about me? What about my life story? Might this patient be interested in what could forge a mutual connection that could improve **our** collective wellness?

Patient: *"Hi Doc, thanks for seeing me. I'm in town from the Isle-of-Man. I know it's short notice!"*

Physician: *"Oh wow, so great to meet you; I just watched a documentary on your country's annual motor-cycle race, and I love your national flag. It is so interesting! I hope you're not here with any leg issues!"*

Patient: *"Ha ha ha, what are the chances that my physician in Chicago would know anything about the Isle-of-Man!"*

Creating a Safe Space: This principle occurs in two phases — simultaneously.

Phase A: Like comics, people assume things about doctors as having all the answers, which can feel challenging on the ego in keeping the "Safe Space." To create a reliable "safe space" for a patient, the doctor can instantly think like a comic, "Who is in front of me, and how do I perceive who is in front of me?" The answers help build natural instincts. For example, by thinking, "I wonder if this patient is Mongolian, the name is so unique." If the physician assumed the patient was Asian, the relationship has little potential for exciting dialogue and the discovery of two unique people.

Phase B: Once the Voice and the Listening are established, and the "safe space" has been created for the patient, the doctor will likely feel more prepared and comfortable navigating any relationship. Thereby setting a tone that honors a patient's personal constraints such as community, socio-economic, and environmental racial bias that are ever-present today. A doctor may like to learn ways to adapt on the fly when new information is revealed, making the patient feel more supported in ways not taught in medical school.

Mrs. Lee: *"Hi Doc, my husband is still smoking, and I tell him five times a day to stop smoking, and he just won't quit!"*

Physician: [responds to husband] *"Mr. Lee, she sure does love you! [to wife] Thank you, Mrs. Lee, for loving your man so much and being so committed to his wellness that you take regular breaks to be a stand for his health because Mr. Lee... she doesn't want to lose you!"*

<natural pause for the room to reflect in silence>

Physician: [responds to husband] *"Mr. Lee, my pops started smoking as a young kid. I asked him why, he said, "Living in a stressful environment was hard, but smoking helped." He always loved Marlboro Reds. Does that happen to be your weapon of choice, too :)? Tell me, when did you start smoking and why? I'd love to hear your story if you have a minute!"*

Summary and Reflection

We are more than our masks, more than our color, and more than our culture. In comedy, we show the united nations within us all through tears and laughter. Please listen fully to "the bagger" within us all; just trying to do a good job at a pace that makes sense. Our sisters and brothers are healing from the last hundred years of chaos. Many of our brothers and sisters barely survived those atrocities or still felt enslaved by them. As we compassionately allow for new healthy ways of overcoming mediocrity — let's consider mediocrity is also perfect!

If you are now ready to start speaking your truth and telling your story using the journaling exercises above, thank you! Consider letting your cellphone battery die and picking up a microphone. As soon as you make someone in your world laugh, you'll feel your real battery charged up to 100%. See you on the road, kiddo!

You're Officially a Stand-Up Comedian!

Journaling Exercise #7 [30 MINUTES]
COMEDY 102: BITCH-IT-TO-ME

Free 30 minute session with me one-on-one. Bring your completed journaling exercises or just bitch at me about my article, either way, it will be fun!

SHARE *YOUR* whole STORY WITH THE WORLD!

Mona Aburmishan

Mona is an international comedian, medium, and emcee who has performed, emceed, and produced comedy shows, competitions, and events in major clubs, theaters, and universities around the world since 2009. Mona is also a sought-after speaker for her experience using stand-up comedy as a transformative method for healing trauma and PTSD for various socio-political topics in the United States, Europe, Africa, and the Middle East. Mona has a Master's in International Development and is fluent in English, German, and Arabic. She performs in these languages while she now works on her Ph.D. Mona became the first Arab and Muslim woman to perform stand-up comedy in the nation's most prestigious institutions: twice at the John F. Kennedy Center and Carnegie Hall!

Mona launched "Class Clowns," a global stand-up comedy, improv, spoken word, and writing workshop for kids and adults of all ages in all environments. It uses the comedy club as a microcosm for leadership, self-expression, face-to-face empowerment, and healing. The workshop is currently running in Chicago and Cape Town, South Africa. "Leadership is more than a person on stage at the microphone; it's everyone else keeping the stage lite and the mic on…otherwise, he's just a comic!"

Mona Aburmishan

Mona Comedy Inc.

40 East 9th Street

Chicago, IL 60605

Mona@MonaComedy.com

www.MonaComedy.com

Bitch-it-to-Me

30 minute free session of bitching to a comedian, where your frustrations are heard, your position is valued, and you feel more connected to the divine.

To book a session visit: MonaComedy.com

Jenni O'Connor

Learning to Love your Body
When It Betrays You

I'm nine years old. I'm hearing the squeak of wheels and clutching the cold rails of a gurney, as I'm rushed into emergency surgery. It's Easter, and I thought I'd be spending the day hunting for eggs and wearing the pretty new dress my mom bought me. Instead, I'm surrounded by worried surgeons and wearing a hospital gown.

For much of my life, I've been pitted against my own body in a seemingly never-ending war. Hospital visits and medications have been a common thread throughout my life. More than once, doctors have crowded around me to see something they'd only read about in textbooks. When this is your reality, it can be easy to see your body as the enemy. So, you might be surprised to know it's become my life's work to not only love my body but to empower others to love their bodies, too.

Poisoned From Within

I woke up vomiting. I'm resting in my room as my parents prepare Easter brunch for our relatives. The pain in my belly grows stronger and shifts to my right side, and we leave for the hospital, just as our relatives arrive.

My appendix isn't in the usual spot, so the surgeons clamp my organs out of the way to locate it. They remove it just in time and send me to recovery, my tiny incision covered with a Band-Aid. However, I'm getting progressively sicker, and they cannot figure out why. Back in surgery, they discover a clamp accidentally tore a hole in my intestines. Five different kinds of bacteria have been seeping into my abdomen, slowly poisoning me. They work quickly to clean up the infection and save my life.

This begins a two-week hospital stay, during which I almost die multiple times. The second incision is much bigger, and we have to change the packing twice daily, even at home. I help, feeling strangely disconnected from my body. Periodically, the surgeon removes any newly-formed scabs so that the wound can heal properly from the inside out. The pain makes me see stars, but yelling out loud isn't acceptable, so I'm quiet. I learn to be silent through pain.

Peak Physical Health

My childhood is filled with medical ups and downs like this. However, by the time I'm in college, I feel like I've finally emerged victorious over my health. I'm an honors student, a student leader, and hold multiple jobs. I take aerobics, run the stairs to my seventh-floor room…I'm even doing "Tae Bo" twice a day. (I probably just dated myself!) I'm at peak physical health and ready to conquer the world.

One night, a sharp pain clutches my chest. I struggle to breathe, telling my friend, "I'm having a heart attack." I'm rushed to an ER, and thankfully, it's *not* a heart attack; it's costochondritis. (And no, you cannot find that at Costco…haha!) I'm told I'm in the beginning stages of fibromyalgia and chronic fatigue syndrome. In a matter of a few days, I go from being healthy and vibrant to not being able to get out of bed or even pick up a pill with my fingers. I start missing classes, lose my public relations job, and almost lose my position as Resident Advisor. My professors graciously work with me, and I complete my finals, defend my thesis, and graduate from college with honors.

Riding the Roller Coaster

I'm now in my mid-20s, and I've landed my dream job. I'm in church, and I look over and see this *gorgeous* guy. Anyone who has been in a church singles group knows hot guys go fast, and I was NOT about to let him get away. So, let me be clear…I picked *him* up.

We date for five months before we get engaged and are married shortly after. I have the job, the husband, the house…I'm back on top of the world! The only thing missing from my wish list is to be a mother. So we decide to start trying. I have to admit; this is the most fun I've had working on something!

I excitedly take a pregnancy test the first month, and it's negative. The second month… negative. I'm told I should relax and try not to worry, but the months start to stack up. I try every fertility-boosting method I can find, from scientific to downright bizarre. Nothing works. I test so obsessively that I actually buy pregnancy tests in bulk. And yes, those you *can* get at Costco!

For two years, we are riding the roller coaster of infertility. I undergo painful procedures and invasive tests. Our sex life has become a medical experiment. Well-meaning but nosy people asked, "When are you having children? You'll make such great parents!" They even teasingly ask if we know "how it works." I laugh with them but go home and weep. I gain weight from depression and comfort eating, which only makes more people ask if I'm finally pregnant. Each month we get our hopes up, and each month I feel betrayed by my body. Scar tissue has completely blocked one of my fallopian tubes, cutting my chances in half. The kicker? It's from my surgeries when I was a child. My past has come back to haunt me.

We discover I have PCOS (Polycystic Ovarian Syndrome), which creates painful ovarian cysts, irregular cycles, and imbalanced hormones, making it even harder to conceive. I begin hormone treatments. Most people don't discuss infertility openly, so I find myself journeying alone through the months of hot flashes and tears. When that is unsuccessful, we're told we can't get pregnant without IVF. Unsure that's the path for us, we begin to research adoption.

In the midst of all of this, my intuition tells me to try one…more… test. And I finally get what I've been wanting…a positive pregnancy test! I so desperately need it to be true that I run out and buy every brand of the test I can find. I take seven more *just* to be sure.

Our beautiful daughter Sabrina is born. Her delivery is easy…I'm even cracking jokes to the doctor between pushes. The hospital plays a lullaby over the speakers when a new baby is born, and my heart swells with pride that this time it's for *my* baby. The hospital nursery nicknames her the Irish Banshee because she's not shy about using her lungs! As she's grown older, she has continued to use her voice fearlessly.

We decide we're so good at this that we should do it a second time. The cycle repeats: two more years of infertility, and we are finally pregnant again. In our gratitude, we name her Eliana. *"God has answered my prayers."* Even during pregnancy, she's entirely different from her sister. A night owl who kicks and dances rhythmically to music, I can feel her tiny fingers tickle me from inside.

Two weeks before my delivery date, my water breaks! I run to the bathroom and discover what I thought was water…is bright red blood. Once again, I'm being rushed to the hospital. It's an hour away, and the baby is not moving. I pray tearfully for just one little flutter to let me know she's OK. Right as we arrive, I feel the tiniest little tickle…she's still with us.

They quickly connect me to monitors, finding both oxygen rates are low. I'm given pitocin, which induces intense contractions. I request a nerve block for pain, but for some reason, it doesn't work. They try a second one and a third one…no luck. I'm told I'll have to endure the super-powered contractions without pain relief.

People fill the delivery room…doctor, nurses, NICU staff, and even residents observing. I'm in transition, and my contractions are now literally disappearing off the charts. My doctor, typically one of the most lighthearted people I know, gravely meets my eyes and says, "Jenni, her heart rate is dropping. You have 90 seconds to get her out." I miraculously find that Warrior Mom strength and deliver her. Relief washes over me…until I realize it's silent. In that room full of people, no one is making a sound; they're hurriedly working. There's fluid in her lungs. I hold my breath until I hear the most beautiful sound in the world...my baby's cry. She's healthy and happy and ***hasn't been silent since!*** I cradle my daughter as the hospital plays its lullaby, and I know she will be a fighter. She's still my sweet, dancing night owl who loves a dramatic entrance!

One More Time

I'm wrangling toddlers when we discover I'm pregnant a third time. We hear our baby's heartbeat and bask in the glow that we *finally* did this on our own. Weeks later, my intuition tells me something is wrong. Trying to ease my nerves, the ER ultrasound tech is laughing and joking...until he's not. Again, it's silent. I know he's not allowed to give a diagnosis, but ask anyway, "Is my baby OK?" He compassionately meets my eyes, and I know. I lie on the gurney in tears, hearing a lullaby play over the speakers. A new baby's entering the world as my baby is leaving it. My body has betrayed me again.

Perfect on the Surface

Between post-miscarriage depression and a severe flare-up of my fibromyalgia, I find myself unable to leave my bed many days. It's a struggle to walk or even breathe without pain, and I use a wheelchair, or my husband literally carries me. I'm unable to work and file for unemployment. They require an interview to establish my level of disability. I get paired with a doctor, who immediately tells me she doesn't believe in fibromyalgia. My claim is denied.

Used to being a high achiever, I start to feel like a failure. I can't work. I'm not a "fun" mom or wife. I can't even create life properly. I rapidly gain weight from medications and immobility. Every moment of every day, I'm in pain. It will be that way for the rest of my life. I start to believe my family would be better off without me and struggle daily with suicidal thoughts. I begin seeing a therapist and tell her I have no idea why I'm depressed. On the surface, I have the perfect life. As we dig down, I realize how much external appearance can differ from what's happening inside. I had embodied the lesson I learned as a child: be silent through pain. I am still engulfed in pain, but now

I'm learning to find my voice; I will not let it consume me...*I will rise above.*

Heels and Chrome...Feels Like Home

My friend, trying to cheer me up, invites me to a pole dancing class. I respond with, "A what?! I'm not sexy. I'm not fit. I'm a good Christian girl... What are you thinking?" I agree to go just to keep her company. Sitting in the lobby, I can hear the whistles and cheers of dancers in the class before ours and wonder what on earth I've gotten myself into! As the women spill out of the classroom after their class, they look so happy and alive. I'm a little jealous.

In class, the instructor invites us to run our hands over our bodies in a loving way. I try and discover just how disconnected I am from my own body — even touching something non-sexual like my arm disgusts me. This body has betrayed me — it has hurt me, it has hurt my children. How can I possibly love it? However, I'm beginning to realize just how much I *need* to.

After our class, we get to watch an advanced class dance. To my surprise, they're all wearing "booty shorts" and sports bras — even women who look like me! I'm shocked at how brazenly they display their imperfections, and then I am quickly ashamed of my judgmental attitude. I realize this space is different. I cheer as they start to dance but quickly find myself watching in hushed awe as they twirl and lift themselves into intricate shapes. My eyes are glued to a woman who is my size. Not only is she doing difficult tricks, but she is moving her body in a way that says, "I love this body. I'm beautiful, and I know it." I find my own hands traveling to my round stomach with its large scars. I want to feel like this. I need to feel like this.

I register for classes and begin the long journey of learning to love my body. At our Level 1 graduation eight weeks later, we each do a solo performance of the routine we've been learning. I'm wearing a sexy outfit, and my belly is out...in public, with scars showing. As the cheers of my classmates buoy me, I sense an almost goddess-like confidence take over. I whip my hair and shimmy my hips, delighting in the way I feel. *I am unstoppable. I am empowered.*

A Phoenix is Born

Pole transforms my life so completely that I decide to open my own studio. Like all journeys, there are high points and low points. I learn lessons and become a stronger person. Before I even have a studio space, I choose the name Studio Phoenix…after the mythical bird that continually regenerates itself after completely burning to ashes. That image resonates with many who are transforming their lives.

Today, Studio Phoenix is a premier Chicago-area pole dance studio. We've helped thousands of women connect with their bodies and find their power…not just within our walls but also in their daily lives. I see students leave toxic relationships, quit unhealthy vices, and find the courage to apply for promotions. A student texts me from her vacation, proudly wearing a bikini and commenting, "This is because of you."

Pole dance is about so much more than just sexy outfits and hair-whips (although they're fun, too!). It teaches us to see our bodies differently…to respect them for what they do, instead of how they look. When we surround ourselves with people who empower each other and actively seek to find the good in others, we are an unstoppable force.

In the years since that first pole dance class, I've worked with thousands of women, both in groups and one-to-one as an embodiment coach. My book, *Rituals for Feminine Power* and its teen edition, outline my methods for transforming your life daily. While those books feature a more long-term approach, I'm going to take this opportunity to introduce three main principles for how you can feel more empowered in your life today.

Principle 1: Connection

Feel Comfortable with Yourself and Others

Disconnection can make us feel isolated. Many of us experienced this with quarantining through Covid-19. While we adapted with Zoom and remote learning, the lack of physical touch and in-person events quickly took its toll.

Humans are pack animals, and we're meant to connect with others.

Your energy also affects people differently when you're disconnected. Have you ever noticed the atmosphere change when someone walks into the room? One person might repel you, causing your red flags to wave, while a different person might feel warm and welcome, like old friends getting reacquainted. Most people experience this powerful energy exchange on a subconscious, gut level. It's hard to explain charisma, but we've all met someone who makes us hang on to her every word.

Before I move on to the next result of not being connected, I want you to notice something. How are you sitting? Are you contained to a small space, tucked away neatly?

Women are persistently sold the message that smaller is better. Our Barbies have impossibly small waists and feet, and our cartoon princesses are a fraction of the size of their princes. Fashion is usually showcased on slim models, and even young girls in acting, dance, and gymnastics are told to lose weight. Women who speak up, express frustration, or take the lead are labeled with demeaning terms. Many of us were reined in with the phrase "like a lady." Sit like a lady, act like a lady, dress like a lady...all of which meant quieter and smaller. However, I want you to be able to **walk into a room and own it.** I want you to fill whatever space you're in, rising to the top.

The solution to disconnection is the connection with others. I know, I know..."Thank you, Captain Obvious!" I promise we'll get to the "how" in a moment. First, I want to touch on connection's possibilities.

Connection helps you:

1. Use your touch to heal others.

2. Transcend other people's limitations.

3. Magnetically attract people.

So, how do we connect? I'll give you an example with a brief story. My apologies to introverts — I'm an introvert by nature, but I stretch myself with this activity. When I'm out in public, I look for ways to compliment strangers… especially women. *A sincere compliment can be transformational.*

I was at a store one day and noticed the cashier had prominent cheekbones. I complimented her, saying they were lovely, and her hands flew to her face. "Oh, do you think so? I've always been so self-conscious about them." I assured her, and we exchanged pleasantries. As I walked out the door, I looked back, and she was gently patting her cheeks with a smile on her face. What if a few kind words could not only help you connect but completely shift someone's way of seeing herself?

Principle 2: Intuition

Trust Your Gut

When we use our intuition, we access a deeper, more primal part of ourselves. If you ignore your intuition, you're lacking in three things…self-knowledge, love, and goals. Without self-knowledge, you don't know who you truly are…your weaknesses or your strong points. Without targeted love, you don't know what methods feed your soul, leaving you feeling frustrated and unheard. Without goals, you don't know where you're going. You don't have a map, and you can't see your future.

The solution is to learn to listen to your intuition. Check-in with your gut when making a decision. How does it feel in your body…like sinking or lifting? What is your reaction when meeting someone before logic and analysis set in? Be present and take the time to focus inward.

When you listen to your intuition, you:

1. Know who you truly are, including weaknesses and strengths.

2. Are empowered to experience love in a way that opens your heart.

3. Know where you are going in life, and have goals that actually work.

Principle 3: Nurturing

Take Care of the Softest Side of Yourself

We all have a vulnerable side that we don't let other people see. If you don't nurture this side, you experience burnout. Burnout is that feeling after a long day of work — maybe you've been in Zoom meetings with that co-worker who can't find mute — and all you can think about is crashing on your couch in comfy sweats and binging mindless TV. Your body isn't meant to run a marathon at a sprint pace. You lose out on the little moments — and those are the ones that you'll regret missing most. ***Lack of nurturing also alienates your inner child.*** You don't take pleasure in little things...there's no joy. Many of us push ourselves too hard, with little room for error or humanity. Our internal monologues are harsh, pointing out every flaw with a sneer. So, when you find yourself being beaten up by your inner critic, I want you to imagine you're speaking to a three-year-old child...would you speak to her the way you speak to yourself?

The solution is to find ways to nurture your body and spirit. I recommend meditation and/or prayer, breath-work, a movement that feels good, delighting your senses, and creativity just for the sake of creativity. Both my podcast (*Ashes to Wings*) and my Instagram (@the_jenni_oconnor) offer ways to incorporate self-care into even the busiest of schedules. One of my favorite exercises is to take a few deep breaths and relax, and then find something you love about yourself unconditionally. Choose something you love...without it being tinted, tucked, or plucked. It doesn't have to be something physical...you may love your loyalty to friends, your hilarious puns, or your mouth-watering cheesecake recipe. For some, this can be difficult at first; but I encourage you to do it regularly, so it becomes easier.

Transformation Takes Effort

So again, the three principles we learned were connection, intuition, and nurturing. You'll find random opportunities to use these, but I also recommend that you incorporate them into your daily life. How many times have you read a book and thought, "Oooh, that was good! Now my life will change!" and then you promptly closed the book and forgot about it? ***Knowledge is not power... applied knowledge is power.*** Transformation takes effort, whether it's through journaling, working with me as a client, or putting sticky notes everywhere with reminders. So, if you need help, reach out to me at JenniOConnor.com. Let's get you living your empowered life *today!*

Jenni O'Connor

Jenni O'Connor is an insightful intuitive who holds space for women to dismantle their emotional armor. As an embodiment coach, she teaches her clients how to listen to the whisper of their bodies before it becomes a scream. Her methods have helped thousands of women to build confidence and feel more connected in body, mind, and emotions. A gold-medalist pole dancer, she owns Studio Phoenix, a women's aerial dance and fitness studio that features fun classes, like pole dance, chair dance, aerial hammocks, and lyra (aerial hoop). Diagnosed with fibromyalgia and chronic fatigue syndrome at age 21, she balances a life between rolling in her wheelchair and flying through the air. Born an introverted wallflower, she has worked hard to overcome her social anxiety and self-doubt to become a confident, powerful woman. She loves helping others develop their best selves! Jenni is an embodiment coach, author, speaker, and podcaster. A certified life coach, somatic coach, and NLP practitioner, she has been a guest expert on podcasts and panels. She has been featured in Costco magazine and Voyage Chicago. You can find her books, Rituals for Feminine Power and Rituals for Feminine Power — Teen Edition, on www.Amazon.com; and her podcast, Ashes to Wings, on your favorite podcast networks.

Jenni O'Connor
Illinois
Jenni@JenniOConnor.com
www.JenniOConnor.com

Empowerment Analysis

We all love archetype quizzes…who doesn't want to know which of the Friends cast they're most similar to? However, while those quizzes are entertaining, they rarely tell you anything of value about who you are and what makes you tick. Jenni O'Connor's free Empowerment Analysis gets to the core of who you are as a person. With handcrafted results tailored to your specific personality, Jenni will show you exactly where you're empowered in life…and pinpoint what needs work.

https://JenniOConnor.com/Empowerment-Analysis

Dr. Lisa Bleicher

Health: A Journey Not A Destination

At the age of 23, I packed up my huge green Plymouth Fury, along with my cat "Kitty," and headed south. I left my parents, siblings, friends, job, and everyone I knew to start a new era in life. Just over a year earlier, I decided and was chosen to become a Chiropractor. I went to one of the smallest schools, recommended to me by my Chiropractor, Arnie Taub (may he rest in peace). Sherman College of Chiropractic turned out to be the best school, although I might just be a little bit biased. This school had the ideal philosophy, not only of Chiropractic but of life as well! Attending Sherman was a challenge, yet it gave me considerable knowledge and many experiences that empowered me, challenged me, opened up my heart, helped me find my passion, put me on a path of continual research, and a lifelong endeavor to uncover the truth of health.

I grew up in a pretty average home. I was blessed with two loving parents. I have a brother and sister, and I am sandwiched in the middle. My mother was a stay-at-home mom, and my father worked in New York City as a lighting technician, mostly for CBS. Our family had many interesting experiences with my dad's jobs over the years. The three of us children were filmed for the movie *Gidget Grows Up*, and we ended up on the cutting room floor. However, the beauty was that it was my first paid job at the age of nine. We were each paid forty-two dollars. We were able to attend the filming of commercials, shows, and films. We met many famous people over the years. My dad was working on the film *Alice's Restaurant*, where we had breakfast with Arlo Guthrie. This was one of the times I was really sick.

A few years prior to that time, I had been diagnosed with severe bronchitis, which became chronic. Even though my parents wanted us to be healthier, they only knew medical care. With chronic bronchitis, I was on antibiotics every time I was sick, which caused chronic constipation. At the age of seven, I also had multiple sore throats. Back in those days, the doctors thought the best treatment was to remove the tonsils. Needless to say, they were removed. I remember my mom telling me a story that the doctor said I would never have sore throats again. However, six weeks after the surgery, I had a sore throat, and my mother was very upset.

My grandmother was a health food store owner, a little wacko, yes true, yet we had an earlier start on looking at health a little bit different than most. She read a lot of books on health that were outside of the norm. We were not allowed to have white sugar or white flour unless it was a very special occasion. I did not like it growing up. However, looking back on it, it really was a start to creating better health. What we learn as children really does stick around into our adult life. What we do with it is a different story.

Growing up in the 1960s and 1970s was a very interesting time. My parents were free thinkers and sort of hippies! When I was 10, our family went on a Peace March in Washington, D.C. We traveled by bus from a local college with friends and a whole bunch of people we did not know. We left super early in the morning. I remember sitting in the back seat with my sister and our friends. When we got to D.C., our parents plopped themselves on the lawn of the White House. My sister was 12, and I was 10. With a few other older friends, we went to march with all the hippies. It was very different then. It was actually safe to be away from your parents, even in a huge peace march. These kinds of experiences with my parents gave me the free spirit that I have and the determination to stand for justice and health freedom for informed choices.

I become a hard worker at a very young age. I learned this work ethic from my dad. I started working as a babysitter at age 11. At the age of 14, I landed a regular part-time babysitting job for a single mom who was a nurse. After school, I would go to her apartment to babysit her two young children so that she could work the middle shift. I had to feed the children, bathe them, help them with their homework, get them to bed, and then do my homework. I would get home very late, get up super early for school and do this three to four days per week. This experience taught me a lot about life, the responsibility of taking care of the kids (which I loved), and still complete my work for school.

When I turned 16, I got a job working at a pharmacy, of all places. Working at this job was a very eye-opening experience in the pharmaceutical world. At this point, I was still getting sick with bronchitis a couple of times a year. I also suffered from chronic headaches and terrible teeth. Back in those days, they always used amalgam fillings, which were filling my head with mercury. I remember a day that I was at the pharmacy. I had just gotten back from the doctor with another antibiotic. I said, "Screw this! I am no longer going to take these meds since I still get sick anyway!" This was a pivotal point in my life. I stopped taking the meds, and the result was the opposite of what most people would think. I started getting sick less often and with less severity. Within two years, I was hardly getting sick at all. I worked at this pharmacy for many years and learned a lot about medications from the drug reps and the pharmacist. One day at work, I asked my boss if he wanted me to put this one med away. He said "No," and I asked, "Why?" He stated the med was being recalled because the medication was killing too many people. Therefore, the pharmaceutical company recalled it. I was shocked! I always thought that medications were safe. I was then taught how medications were tested. They were allowed to kill a few people, and the meds were still deemed safe. The medication was then made available to the public. If they exceeded a certain percentage of deaths, they would then recall the medication. This led me to think that there is more to health than taking medications.

This became the triangle time of my life: College, home, and work at the pharmacy. They were all ten minutes apart from each other. I was going to college full-time, working full-time, and hanging with the girlfriends full-time.

I was still living at home when I did my undergrad at William Paterson College (now University). At the age of 19, when I was a sophomore in college, my sister started having severe migraines. Limited to her knowledge of traditional medical care, my mom took my sister to the doctor. He stated that she was having cluster migraines and that there was nothing he could do for her except medication. We were trying to stay away from meds at this point in our health journey as a family. The migraines were really severe, and we did not know what to do. My sister's boyfriend at the time said, "That's it, I am going to take you to our family chiropractor!" We were like, family chiropractor? Back in the day, chiropractic was frowned upon. They were considered the scary doctors! Needless to say, my sister went to the chiropractor. She started getting adjusted, her migraines started going away, and they became less severe and less common. The changes in my sister's health were pretty dramatic, for which we were thankful. She was not fun to live with when she was suffering from the migraines.

My sister was very excited that her adjustments helped her get her life back. She even got my mom to go to the chiropractor. She had been suffering from severe low back pain for a few years. The doctors told her all they could do was for her to have spinal surgery. She refused and endured pain and all. She would sneeze and land on the floor because the pain was so bad at times. This was gut-wrenching for us to see. My mom ended up having a permanent condition, which was a deteriorated disc between her third and fourth lumbar vertebrae. Even with this permanent condition, my mom's low back pain decreased tremendously. Over time, she became mostly pain-free and rarely had a flare-up. Then my sister and Mom harped on me to go to the chiropractor. I fought it for some time and then finally gave in. I figured I would go, check it out, and see how and why they were getting better.

Just before I turned 20, I started to go to the chiropractor. I learned that chiropractic was not about fixing people's back problems and headaches. The first chiropractic patient actually regained his hearing from a chiropractic adjustment. I thought that was very interesting and that there was something to this chiropractic adjustment. I kept going to get adjusted weekly. I started to see that my energy levels were changing, which helped me endure my crazy schedule. Remember, I was working full-time, going to college full-time, hanging with the girls full-time, and volunteering at the college's Help Line. At this point in my college career, I was a psychology major. I was planning to become a child psychologist, primarily abnormal psych. However, I was starting to get into health and still wanted to help children. Psychology seemed like the path. In the meantime, my chiropractor, Dr. Arnie, started encouraging me to become a chiropractor. I was resistant at first until I heard him do a talk about chiropractic and kids. I will never forget that day. I was sitting with my mom in Dr. Arnie's office. He was explaining the birth process and how the bones in the baby's spine could move out of place and interfere with the nerve system. I got tingles all up and down my arms. I had a sensation I had never felt before. I knew I needed to go to chiropractic school. I could take care of kids!

At this point, I only had two more courses to complete for my undergrad degree. This would allow me to complete all of the pre-requirements I needed for chiropractic school. I did this in my fifth year of undergrad. I graduated in the summer of 1982, and I left for chiropractic school that August. I moved to Spartanburg, South Carolina, to attend Sherman College of Chiropractic. I went to this school because my mentor, Dr. Arnie, said that it was the best school to attend. He said that I would learn chiropractic philosophy correctly and completely at this school. I am very glad that I listened. It changed my life.

The first class, Chiropractic Philosophy 101, was an eye-opener since we were taught about creation. When you think about health and how the body works, you definitely need to know about the creation of it. All living things have their own intelligence called Innate Intelligence or inborn wisdom. In humans, this Innate Intelligence is what controls how our bodies work. Our bodies are very complex. There are hundreds and hundreds of functions that are working in our bodies 24/7. Our bodies are so complex and SO intelligent that they even create life from the union of two cells! It is absolutely amazing and really unbelievable that our Innate Intelligence is smarter than any man, woman, or scientist. We keep discovering more and more of this intelligence and more functions of the body. Who knows how much is still unknown.

This Innate Intelligence is what tells our bodies what to do and how to do it. For example, it tells our heart how to beat for each and every situation. If you are resting, it is slower, versus if you are running, it would beat faster. This is just one function out of hundreds and hundreds of other functions. Therefore, what controls all these functions? Innate Intelligence uses the brain as the master controller. It tells your heart how to beat, your lungs how to breathe, your stomach how to digest, your cells grow, and what type of cell is needed. These are just a few examples. The brain communicates with every part of you through the nerve system. Chiropractic works on the spine to make sure this nerve supply from the brain goes to all the various body parts to its fullest capacity. This is the power that keeps us functioning at our best. Chiropractic keeps that power flowing to each and every cell, giving us the chance to function to our fullest capacity creating optimal health. This is how complex we are. It is absolutely amazing.

Function is the most important thing in our lives: When all the functions of the body are operating at their fullest capacity, it is optimal health! Health is how our body works. It is NOT about whether we are symptomatic or not. For instance, right now, can you feel whether your body is creating a healthy cell or a cancer cell? Can we feel if the heart is working at 100% or 80%? No, we cannot. Health is not about how we feel. It is about how well the body is working. Here is another example: Let's say you eat rotten food. What usually happens (hopefully) is that you vomit, have diarrhea, or both! It is not fun, and there are many symptoms. This actually shows that you are healthy because your body is getting rid of the poison! It is a normal response of the body to protect itself. We have many systems and functions in us that protect us. The one most common that people know of is the immune system.

I found how the brain, nervous system, and human body are amazing and complex, yet very logical. It made me aware of the intelligence inside of each and every one of us. However, it baffled me why people always interfere with this intelligence. For every little symptom or expression, a pill is popped, a shot is given, and toxic treatments are given. However, the body is just expressing itself. This is where I became obsessed to keep learning more and more. I started researching vaccines and how they were developed. I wanted to know the ingredients of vaccines, medications, foods, and environmental toxins. I was curious about how these things were affecting our bodies and why we develop what we are experiencing in life and health. I started my quest, and maybe that will be my next book.

I graduated from chiropractic school in August 1985. I moved back home temporarily to take boards and to decide where I was going to open my own practice. I moved to Jim Thorpe, Pennsylvania, in 1986 and opened my practice that December. It has been a blessing to teach people about what health is, that it comes from within, and to adjust their spines to make sure they are getting the proper nerve supply to function to their fullest. One of the biggest things I learned on this journey is that we are all different. We are all unique in many ways. We are just as different on the inside as we are on the outside. What works for one might not work for another. I have had many clients get rid of their back pain, while others did not. I have had two women conceive after nine or ten months of chiropractic care when nothing they previously tried for years led to conception. Chiropractic was founded on a deaf person who regained his hearing, not a low back person. Chiropractic is about making sure the nerve supply is flowing to keep us functioning optimally. If the body can heal it, it will.

After having my first child, I had blood in my stool and was a bit freaked out. I went to the doctor who did an extensive intake, asking many questions like nationality, what country my parents and grandparents were from, as well as health questions, which I found very interesting. I had mentioned that both my parents were first-American born in our family and that my dad was Jewish. The internist made a statement that Jewish people have a high incidence of lactose intolerance (which my dad's cousin actually did). Well, the Doc scoped me and told me to eat more salads, which I thought was funny. Even though I was eating pretty healthy, this experience put me on a path to change what I was doing in my diet and stress levels that could have affected this issue. I did some research and decided to go dairy-free. I went totally dairy-free, and even no-whey, which is some breads. Within two weeks, I ended up having normal bowel movements for the first time in my life! That chronic constipation for 25 plus years went away. I then started down another path to understand more about food and what it does.

I became the ingredient Nazi! Every time I would take the kids grocery shopping, and they wanted some junk, I would ask them to read the ingredients and see where the real food was. I learned about additives, chemicals, labeling, and how it can be deceptive. I also learned how they spray packaging with chemicals to preserve them, so they would not have to list it in the ingredients. It is so important to eat real food for the proper nutrition and to keep the toxins out. Our bodies need very specific nutrients for the functions which keep us healthy.

The most amazing blessings I have ever had was to birth and raise my three children, Tristan, Shane, and Abigail. My children were not raised on shots and medications. They were raised by turning on True Health from the beginning. They were checked for nerve interference from birth. I was able to teach them what I knew and as I learned. By working with them and their health, physically, mentally, emotionally, and spiritually, it has allowed them to grow up into amazing human beings. They have also taught me much and still do. They have empowered me to be the best me! Life is a blessing, and we need to turn the volume up every chance we can get. We need to turn life on daily.

> *"God has given us all the pieces required to achieve optimal function/health but has left us to put the pieces together."*

Learning that health starts from within and everything we do (or do not do) to it from the outside-in also has an effect on our bodies internally. Health is all of what we do physically, mentally, emotionally, and spiritually. It all works together. All of our functions, body parts, and nervous system work together. Chiropractic is the foundation, yet there is much to learn and apply from the outside-in. I have blossomed into serving people to learn how to shift from the treatment "fix it" kind of model into True Health Care. True Health Care is where you and your body are most important, where you take care of it every single day and where you learn what is best, what to put in it, on it, or what to do with it. Having the proper nerve supply keeps those functions strong. We feed those functions from the outside-in with water, sleep, nutritious foods, movement, exercise, prayer and meditation, mind care, love, and hugs!! My clients being guided on their journey has helped them move from functional to optimal living in joy, peace, and ease.

Thank you for letting me share my story with you. It is very interesting how experiences shape us and guide us on our life journey. I am here to serve with hugs and God bless.

Dr. Lisa Bleicher

Dr. Lisa Bleicher is a Doctor of Chiropractic and owner of Family Chiropractic, aka Jim Thorpe Chiropractic Center. Dr. Lisa, who has her BA in Psychology, is also honored to be a Life Wellness coach who helps women entrepreneurs heal by taking them from a treatment model of health care to one of True Health through changes in their Healthstyles to live a life of joy and ease. Her passion is to speak internationally, shifting the current healthcare model to one of True Health. Dr. Lisa is a speaker and health freedom advocate and is addicted to research and learning. In fact she is currently studying for her Certification in Brain Health.

Dr. Lisa served on the Chiropractic boards of the Chiropractic Federation of Pennsylvania and the International Federation of Chiropractic Organizations.

Dr. Lisa has been on quite a few non-profit boards. The longest-running was with the United Way of Carbon County, being President for four years and on the board for ten years. She served in many capacities with the PTA while her children were in school. She served twelve years running the book fairs for all grades. She served as Committee Chair on her boy's local Boy Scout Troop. Her proudest achievement is being Mom to her three amazing children: Tristan, Shane, and Abigail.

Dr. Lisa Bleicher
Family Chiropractic
716 North Street
Jim Thorpe, PA 18229
570-242-2466
DocLisa@ptd.net
www.DoctorLisaB.com
www.LinkedIn.com/in/Dr-Lisa-Bleicher-5706aa10
www.Facebook.com/Lisa.Bleicher.1

---

10 Tips to Take Your Health from Functional to Optimal

Ten simple health style changes to take to get you on the journey of a health transformation.

www.DoctorLisaB.com/10-Top-Tips

Carmela Raimondi

A Diamond in the Rough

The hospital waiting room phone rang. The nerves in my stomach had a painful twinge. The results of my husband, Nick's biopsy were in. Our lives would be forever changed by this phone call. I picked up the phone, and the voice on the other end explained that Nick had an aggressive form of cancer and that we would need to schedule emergency surgery immediately. I felt like the world had stopped but was racing at the same time. I was falling apart. However, I needed to be strong because he needed me.

Never in my wildest dreams did I imagine that I would face a series of problems like this in my life. And then, not only would I figure them out, but I would have the opportunity to share my journey with others in a book of my own.

But here I am.

And here you are.

My hope is for you to feel just as empowered as I did as I share my story with you.

Here Is My Story:

I grew up in a strict Italian household in Chicago. My parents were immigrants, so we spoke Italian in our house. Both of my parents were hard-working, and our grandmother took care of my siblings and me while they worked. The relationship that I have with my parents and siblings has always been close. Both parents have always pushed me to be the best version of myself that I could be. My mom is one of the classiest women that I know. I have always wanted to be just like her. The energy and the strength that she has is unbelievable. Since I was a little girl, I can remember always wanting to be by my father's side. He is what every man should be: a hardworking, loving man who poured his greatness into his children. Before retiring, my dad was a foreman at a construction company. He would let me help him with his timesheets, so I would feel important. From that experience, I gained a passion for the construction industry. However, I did not realize that I would spend more than 30 years running my own construction company.

Diamond Beginnings

I first met my husband, Nick, when I was a teenager. It was a whirlwind romance, and we got married when I was young. We were blessed with two beautiful children, Angela and Nick. We could not have been happier. We had a wonderful life together, vacationed, did many fun things with our children, and made many beautiful memories.

My first job was working in a hair salon. As a young girl, I had dreamed of becoming a hairdresser. When I had an allergic reaction to the chemicals, it was very emotional because I wanted it so badly. However, I finally realized that hairdressing was not for me, so I adapted. When I was offered a job by a close friend who managed a travel agency, I decided to give it a go. I thought that working in travel could be interesting. And it was.

Nick and I discussed opening our own business in the concrete construction industry because of Nick's work experience. We felt like it was the right time. Even though I loved working at the travel agency, I was enthusiastic about this change. We did have some resistance from people who were skeptical but decided to jump in with both feet. We agreed that I would oversee the office while Nick handled the fieldwork. I went into it not really knowing much about running an office. I ended up learning through intuition, dedication, and hard work. The business took off and was running well. We found that we were not only a great team at home but also meshed well at work. Life was wonderful.

Troubled Times

Six years into our business, things were going great. Business was good, and life was incredibly positive. We had even bought a property for the business. Out of nowhere, Nick started having back issues. After extensive tests, he was diagnosed with osteosarcoma, which is a form of cancer. I felt like my world was crumbling around me and that I had no control. Nevertheless, we kept the business going in a positive direction. Groundbreaking for our building had commenced. We were both thankful for my brother's assistance in the building process and for always being there for us.

Nick required multiple surgeries, chemotherapy, and radiation treatments over the next few years. I was back and forth to the hospital, sometimes traveling around the country for his treatments, raising my children, and running the business. My daughter, Angela, was really a pillar during this chaotic time. She helped with her younger brother and in any way that she could to support our family. One night, I had a dream where Saint Padre Pio appeared to me. Although I did not know who he was at the time, the dream really stuck with me.

In 1999, things started looking better. Nick was in remission, and we had the opportunity to vacation to Italy. Both of us, being religious, decided that part of our trip would be well-spent attending some of the religious ceremonies there. However, being able to visit the church from my dream was a deeply spiritual event in my life. It strengthened my connection with God and created the bond with my preferred Saint Padre Pio. I am grateful for this profound experience because it gave me the strength for what was to come.

The following year they found another spot of cancer, which was aggressive. Nick had to go for special treatments in California. I was remotely running my business between treatments and caretaking while still raising two young children. I cannot believe how much responsibility was on my shoulders. However, I found the strength to work it out. My parents and some close family members traveled with us. Some close friends and family from

San Diego also helped us through this difficult time. I always felt like God was giving me the courage to continue. We returned home, but unfortunately, they were unable to stop the spread. Nick passed in late 2000.

Cloud of Grief

Sometimes you're on autopilot. You're going forward, but not sure how you're getting there. I believe that God "took the wheel" during this time and gave me the strength to go on. There were times that I questioned myself. I had always had my husband by my side to help me make decisions. I was now on my own, having to decide everything for myself. This was one of the hardest things that I had to overcome.

My business kept me focused and putting one foot in front of the other. It became my focal point, so I could pour myself into it. I was able to build it up for my children to have this legacy, so they would have this piece of their father to hold on to.

The Tough Get Going

After Nick passed, I had to decide what I was going to do. Was I going to sell everything? I thought that my business would not be able to continue after I lost him. I was feeling depressed and angry. I had many goals and felt it all crumbling around me. I felt powerless like I needed my husband to make them happen. I thought life was over for me.

However, I slowly found my confidence by getting up every morning and doing what needed to be done. I said to myself, NO WAY, I am not giving up. Even if I had a dark day, I would always tell myself that I could do it and that I HAD to do it.

After much thought and deliberation, I decided that I wanted to continue the business that Nick and I had started. I figured that I would give it a chance, even though this was a "man's field." I would give it all I had and see what would happen. I took a big risk taking over as president and becoming a business owner. A woman in a male-dominated industry is like a diamond in the rough.

Looking back on this time, people always tell me how strong I am. However, I always just thought of it as putting one foot in front of the other. I now see that it was the beginning of my empowerment. I did feel lost at times, but my kids were really my driving force. They were my "WHY" to get me through this period of my life. It was incredibly challenging to be a single, young mom. I watched those around me going home to their full families while I went home alone with my children and my responsibilities. It was stressful to own a business, deal with those pressures, and to deal with my grief. A lump of coal turns into a diamond under pressure. This time of my life caused my growth, giving me wisdom, courage, and strength.

My brother-in-law had been working for me for some time, and Nick had prepared him for the eventuality that I would need help, should I decide to continue the business. He took over as Field Manager, helping me greatly until my son was old enough to assume that responsibility.

Months after Nick passed, I had a General Contractor ask me, "What are you waiting for? You are a 'Women's Business Owner,' and you should get your minority certification!" I immediately started researching. While it did take some time and effort, I eventually became a certified DBE (Disadvantage Business Enterprise) through Metra. I also got my WBE (Women's Business Enterprise) certification from the WBENC (Women's Business Enterprise National Council) and my respective certifications as a WBE through DuPage and Cook Counties. These certifications really helped my business to grow and were a springboard. I was working with general contractors, who I might not have worked with otherwise. The amount of work that I was doing for the state increased, which more than doubled sales. I had to hire additional employees to keep up with the growth we were experiencing.

In addition to Rai Concrete, I also rent out properties. I have multiple rental units and rental spots, which I am actively marketing.

I would have never thought that my life could continue after what I went through. I believe in the power of positive thinking. I believe that if you are positive, everything will work out in the end.

Happiness 2.0

Life has a way of getting away from you at times. It was not easy for me. I had good days and bad days. I did have family and friends who reached out, but at some point, life starts to return to routine. I never thought about finding love again, but it found me.

My brother is a musician and introduced me to his friend, Marco, who is also a musician. I would have never known that I could meet another man who I would want to marry. But I did. I feel like I have been blessed for a second time. Marco not only understands my loss but also accepts and loves my family the same way that I do. This means the world to me. He balances me and motivates me to achieve my goals.

My daughter Angela is truly amazing. She helped with her brother while going to both high school and beauty school to follow her own passion of becoming a hairdresser. She also worked in my construction office. My son Nick is a driven individual, and at times, it feels like his dad is back. He really took the initiative to learn about our company and help grow it. He has a strong work ethic and has relieved some of the pressures from the outside operations. I am immensely proud of the adults that my children have become. I know that I succeeded as a parent by looking at who they are today.

In addition to finding love again, I have gained a beautiful family. My relationships with my son-in-law, James, and daughter-in-law, Katie, are like I have gained another son and daughter. I currently have seven beautiful grandchildren. My children, my grandchildren, and my husband, Marco, are my LIFE and my WORLD.

Thankful

I am very thankful for the family and friends who supported my children and me through the tragic time in my life. Without some of them, I do not think my life and/or business would have weathered this storm. I would like to thank all my family and friends, my siblings, and especially the people who helped me personally and with my business. Thank you so much for your love and support. I love you all so much!

Due to the things that I have gone through in my life, I feel that now I am a stronger, more empowered person. I believe that I am closer with God and that He gave me the strength to go on in my life. I am thankful for having this spiritual relationship.

Diamonds of Wisdom

I went through so much. I genuinely believe that my children and my bond with God are what got me through the most difficult time. They allowed me to continue in my life and in my business. I did have my ups and downs and felt depressed. Looking back, there are times where I cannot believe that I continued. However, I am glad that I did because I really love what I do and love each of my businesses. They are my passion.

People have asked me, how do I do it? How are you capable of being a woman and running a construction business on your own? The implication that I couldn't do this because I was a woman lit a fire in me. This made me feel more motivated to prove what I am capable of accomplishing and that I am strong enough to achieve my goals. I became empowered and dedicated to proving my doubters wrong, and SO CAN YOU!

I did this by setting long-term and short-term goals for myself. I also made sure that I took the steps needed to accomplish those goals. The short-term goals are rewarding in that you can feel the sense of accomplishment more often. However, the long-term goals have given me a bigger feeling of pride since they are harder to achieve. I did not succeed at every single goal that I set. However, I didn't let that defeat me. My advice to you is to set goals and then follow through on them.

I believe that when you go through something bad in life, it makes you stronger. I would like to encourage you that if you stay strong, you can do it! Don't let anybody convince you that you can't do something with their negativity because YES, YOU CAN! Be resilient! Don't let challenges beat you. When life seems too difficult to continue, just breathe and tell yourself that you can do it. I knew that I had to continue for my "WHY" (which for me was my kids). This kept me going to reach my goals. Find your "WHY" — your motivation. If necessary, make visual reminders of your "WHY" and put them in places that your eyes will fall on frequently to help keep you on track.

I want to empower you. Whether you are going through a tragedy, difficulties, or obstacles, do not give up. Life can not only go on, but there is a light at the end of the tunnel. Reach for your goal. Do not let anything or anyone stand in your way. You must be your own biggest cheerleader. I am always looking into ways of empowering those around me to overcome mediocrity. I believe that what you give off, you get back. I never gave up. I kept on going, no matter how difficult life seemed.

There are good times and bad. I was able to pick myself up during the tough times because I love and believe in what I do. Always remember that no matter what happens, anything is possible. It is about your mindset. If you believe it, you can do it. If you keep a positive outlook, life will be just fine. I will never stop motiving and empowering or making people feel good about their goals and accomplishments. This is a small part that I can do to make this world a better place.

Health and Wellness

As you can imagine, the experience of losing my husband and the pressures of handling everything on my own was very taxing on my body. I was tired, easily stressed, and always felt drained. I found myself not eating well and not sleeping right. I knew that I wanted to find a solution. I thought to myself, "I learned to run a construction company and learned to manage my family. I can learn how to deal with my health." And I did. What I didn't realize was how easy it would be when I found a system.

In 2014, I was approached by a health and wellness coach, who introduced me to a nutritional system. I almost immediately knew that this product was a good fit for me. After only a few weeks on the program, I noticed a difference in how I felt. My energy levels were increasing, and it changed my life. I never realized just how drained I felt until I had this new burst of energy. I was eating right, losing weight, and even enjoying working out. This made me want to share this with my family and friends and eventually network out. It made it easy to quickly advance within the company.

What my friends and I love is the variety of products. There are meal replacement shakes, which can be a tool for weight loss, muscle building, or a combination of the two. There are also meal replacement bars, a metabolism booster, anti-aging collagen, snacks, an intermittent fasting system for nutritional rebalancing, and also products to help with stress relief and health maintenance. These products can help balance your lifestyle, whatever your age. Child obesity is at the highest rate it has ever been. Anyone can utilize this product.

I love coaching people and helping them with health and wellness. I always joke that if I were to be reincarnated, that I would become a doctor. Life is short. We need to stay healthy to appreciate it. My husband had talked about trying the product but was skeptical. After a negative doctor appointment, he came to me and said that he would like to give the products a try. I was excited to share this product that I was so passionate about. After a short time of being on the product, he noticed that he felt a change. He had more energy and was feeling better. He was able to tighten his belt because he was losing inches. When he went for a recheck, he had lost approximately thirty pounds, and the doctor was able to reduce his medication. At his next recheck, he had lost a total of forty-five pounds! The improvement of his quality of life was the biggest reward.

The wonderful thing about taking care of yourself is that it impacts those around you. A young family member saw the adults around her transforming. While she was sleeping in and not able to get out of bed, her mom was changing, getting up, and going to the gym in the morning. She wanted that, and she also wanted to lose weight. After starting the products, she started to feel more energy, which resulted in her going to the gym. She lost pounds and inches and ultimately was recognized by the company for a huge transformation.

Don't Wait

You may be going through similar struggles as mine or have your own set of challenges. Regardless, life is too short. Nobody else is going to do it for you, so you must reach for it yourself. Your health impacts not only you but also your loved ones. These products really helped my family and me. They might also be able to help you. Having survived loss, I can tell you that no matter what your struggle is, your health is the most important. If you don't have your health, nothing else matters.

What a wonderful gift to be able to empower and motivate people and make money while doing it! It can be life-changing. I would love to be able to share it with the entire world. It's not only about the products. There are relationships and friendships that you build and life lessons that you learn by becoming part of the community.

To learn more about how I can help you with your health and wellness, contact me at CarmelaRaimondi63@gmail.com or visit my website at https://linktr.ee/CarmelaRaimondi

Carmela Raimondi

Carmela is a very motivated individual who runs several businesses. She is the President of Rai Concrete construction company, with over 30 years of experience in the construction industry. She has earned her DBE, WBENC, Cook County WBE, and DuPage County WBE Minority certifications. These endorsements have empowered her to take her business to the next level, furthering her goals. Carmela is driven to succeed and never sits still. She is also passionate about health and wellness since losing her late husband to cancer.

Carmela is a Crystal Executive Entrepreneur with a health and wellness company. She wants to be able to help people stay healthy, get fit, provide age rejuvenation, and become financially well. She is dedicated to inspiring people to become the healthiest version of themselves while creating an additional income. Carmela is always looking into empowering those around her. Even in the darkest times, Carmela has never given up. She just kept on going to reach her goals, always staying confident in herself.

Carmela has a close bond with her family. No matter how hectic life gets, there is always time for her loved ones. She enjoys spending time with her current husband, two adult children, son-in-law, daughter-in-law, and seven amazing grandchildren. She is also very close with her parents, siblings, and family. She is a very spiritual individual and thanks God daily for giving her the strength and courage to be the person she is today. Carmela resides in the northwest suburbs of Chicago with her husband. She also enjoys cooking, good food, good wine, dancing, music, and attending her husband's musical events.

Carmela Raimondi
Rai Concrete, Inc.
Nicolangela Building, LLC.
Health and Wellness and Financial Freedom
CarmelaRaimondi63@gmail.com
www.CarmelaRaimondi.com
https://linktr.ee/CarmelaRaimondi

Rachel Cope

It Was One of Those Life Defining Moments

I still remember the sound of her screaming. In a single moment, my whole world turned upside down. I was four years old, maybe five, relaxed and peacefully sleeping. **Her screaming woke me.** It was terrifying, the kind you never forget, that shakes you to the core.

The door burst wide open. My mother stood there looking terrified for her life as my father chased her down the corridor. The next thing I knew, her head was slamming into the metal bunk bed right next to my brother and me. *I really thought he was going to kill her.* Now, I was terrified too.

I don't remember too much about that night. I'm sure it's buried deep down somewhere in here, but I do remember those screams and the sound of her head slamming into the metal bars. I also remember being very scared and thinking, *"I don't know what to do, and my mummy should know what to do. Someone help me!"* There I was, a young child, and in a heartbeat, my life was turned upside down, changed forever. I haven't slept through the night since.

A five-year-old child had decided that she was helpless because standing in front of her was her mother, helpless, wanting two small children to rescue her. We left not long after that.

It Was One of Those Life-Defining Moments That Defined the Next 40 Years of My Life.

I was the youngest of five. It's all a bit blurry time-wise. Two hundred miles north from one small town in the UK to another. I don't remember much about that time in my life as it has become distorted over the years, but some memories have stuck with me. I was sitting on a huge grassy field, in a new and strange school, knowing no one and feeling so very, very alone. *I still remember the smells.*

We lived in these tall buildings that they called flats. They had giant garbage disposals that went from the top floor to the bottom. I remember the smell of the crabs that were caught by the local fisherman, which they left to dry on top of these garbage disposals. *The smell was terrible!* It haunted me for years, and I've never been able to eat seafood of any kind. Not once!

I don't know how long we lived there. In my mind, I made up that it was a year we were gone. However, I'm not sure how long it really was. We never really talked about the experience. We were good at fighting in our family but not talking. When things happened in our family, no one ever mentioned them again. For now, we were living back at home with both mum and dad. I don't know what the truth is. **I just know I didn't ever truly feel like I fit in again.**

Life seemed so hard all of a sudden. My whole life became an experience of being very scattered and chaotic over the years. I was terrified and worried on the inside all the time. I constantly felt anxious about everything, alone and aloof, yet I had a sense that *my true potential could be much more and that I was not living up to my full potential.*

The Opposite of Empowered.

I didn't even know there was a word called **empowered** or that my life was the complete opposite of that. I certainly wasn't surrounded by anyone who was empowered in their lives or that could show me how to empower mine. The only exception was maybe my godmother, and even then, I didn't realize it was OK to talk to her or anyone else. We were raised in the conversation, *"Keep everything behind closed doors."*

My Life Had Become About Survival.

By the time I was eleven, it had become clear to me that the world really wasn't safe, and I was certainly not wanted here. I was mainly a loner. I was always trying to make friends and fit in. It was tough for me to make friends, not to mention keep them. I was scared a lot and was starting to become scared of all kids/adults. I never felt I belonged anywhere or that anyone ever liked me. No matter what I did, I never felt enough. I did, however, constantly feel like my only job was to survive and make it through another day.

I'd become terrified of the kids in the neighborhood. They were always yelling at me and telling me to go away. *Why couldn't I get along with others?* Every day I walked to school wondering if today would be the day I didn't make it home. **I felt like I was leaving one war zone to go into another.** I was lonely and afraid.

The walk to school was just under two miles. It might as well have been a hundred. I discovered there was a shortcut across a field along the way. However, getting from one side to the other seemed like a huge risk. Would I be able to make it without other kids finding me and bullying me, and hurting me? Could I make it to school without getting followed by other kids? Some days I made it across the field and onto the bus, and some days I didn't. Nothing was different upon leaving school.

The bus had become unsafe. I'd climb on, and the bullies would climb on too. I'd get off, and they'd get off too. There was constant name-calling, taunting, bullying, and shaming. It was *relentless*. My life had become mediocre and numb. **I had become a victim to everything that was going on around me.**

I used the same mediocre strategy I used to get home everywhere. It involved getting to school alive, making it through the day, and getting back home safely. I got out the door to school again the next day, just to do it all again.

I Lost My Ability to Believe in Myself.

Somewhere around twelve or thirteen, the "I'm stupid" conversation got really loud. All I'd known to that point was that I was smart. I'd been in the Gifted and Talented program at school. A-student up to that moment and never doubted that I was great at whatever I set out to do. I could be and do anything I wanted in my life. *Suddenly, that was gone.*

I remember sitting in Biology, halfway back in the classroom. The teacher was short, with dark hair and a no-nonsense personality. I don't know what that particular class was even about, but I do remember the moment I started thinking, *"Oh my god, I don't know what she's talking about. I have no clue what's going on here."* It was the first time in my life I had not been able to understand the lesson. At that moment, I decided: **"I was stupid"** and **"No one must ever find out."** It became the beginning of the end of what was possible for me for years.

Suddenly, every class I had ever loved got confusing. I believed I was not smart and that there was something wrong with me. All of my classes, including physics, French, and mathematics, were no longer something I loved. Instead, they were something to dread. I became quiet in class and never spoke up. I began failing classes. I went from being an A student to a mediocre C student.

Nothing had changed. *I just lost my ability to believe in myself.* I was listening to my own self-doubt, and I didn't know it. It seemed very real to me and stayed that way until I was 45 years old.

The "Joy" of Being Fifteen.

Boy were *those* the years I remember there being so *much more* to deal with.

Somewhere along the way in high school, I finally started to feel like I had made a friend or two. Yet not a single friend ever stuck around for long. I was always striving to be in with the "in crowd" and not appreciating the friends that were right under my nose.

I made friends with one girl, named Karen, who I had almost idolized in middle school. In the mornings, I would go to her house, and we would walk to school together. When I arrived, she would be drying her pretty blonde hair.

She was very popular, pretty, blonde, and had boobs. She was everything I wasn't. She seemed so much more grown-up and confident than me. *I had her on a high pedestal.*

Another Pivotal Moment in My Life.

Karen was dating a guy named Mike. He had dark hair and was the DJ at the local discos. I don't know how old he was, but I knew he was waaaay older than us. *I was so naive back then.*

Mike had a friend named Will. Will was a big guy but wasn't very attractive to me. All I could see was that he was overweight, and I didn't want to date a guy who was overweight. I was a girl with standards!

There were many mornings when we would walk to school, and there would be the boy drama. *"Mike looked at this girl. Mike talked to that girl."* She'd share their fights, their make-ups, and the make up sex. And then it happened. I said something that changed my life for the rest of my school days and beyond.

We were walking to school as usual on a cool, dry late spring day. Karen was sharing one of her many dramatic stories of fighting with Mike. I opened my mouth and said, *"You know, what I think we all should do, Karen? I think we should all be gay, and then we wouldn't have any boy problems ever again!"* I was actually quite proud of myself. I thought it was a really funny thing to say and that she'd think so too.

I didn't think any more about it until we left school that day. I knew once again that my life had changed. It was not for the better. It was just when I was starting to feel like I was getting the hang of this school and *friend* thing.

"Rachel's gay!" *"Hey!!!!! Did you know Rachel's a lesbo?!"* **It was relentless.**

The laughter echoed all around me, getting louder and louder. I felt ashamed, betrayed, confused, and wanted to run away. Did the whole school know? I was convinced that they did. It didn't matter if it was true or not. She had betrayed me, and now the whole school thought I was gay.

I Will, If You Will.

My bestie, Michelle, and I were sitting in her bedroom. We'd been chatting about her boyfriend Will and my new "boyfriend" Jason. She'd been dating Will for several years and was thinking about having sex with him. I don't know which one of us created *"I will, if you will."* We definitely made that pact. I'd met Jason five minutes ago. Well, maybe not five minutes, but you get what I mean.

Fast forward, and I was alone in a not-cool situation, with a tall, skinny, long dark-haired kid called Jason. I was standing in his mother's bedroom. I remember it was a simple room, and the bed wasn't made. The sheets were an off-white color. It wasn't romantic. It didn't feel nice. It just felt sterile, although nothing about this room was sterile.

Looking back, I didn't feel honored by myself or this boy. I don't remember how old he was nor what the conversations were that led to this moment. He and I had somehow agreed to have sex. Now, here I was in his mother's bedroom. I was alone. I didn't know how to say no. I didn't know I had a choice. My parents never allowed us to say no, so it never occurred to me that I could.

My dad raised us that our **"Word was everything."** However, he never taught me how to revoke my word. How that would have changed everything, being empowered to say, "I've changed my mind." You gave your word, and you did what you said. *"Your name is all you have, Rachel. Don't ruin your reputation by being dishonorable."*

I went through with it. I laid there as stiff as a board and waited for it to be over. Was I an empowered young woman in this situation? Hell no, I wasn't. Did this affect my sex life in the future? Hell yes, it did!

At that moment, I gave up my belief that what I wanted mattered and that I had any say in my life going how I said. I gave up on what I wanted and deserved being honored as a young woman. Everything I wanted in my life became unattainable at that moment because I decided I didn't matter. I had no ability to say no, and you had to do what you said you would, even if you didn't want to.

I made a promise, and *"You have to do what you said you would do"* started a pattern that stayed with me for the next 30 years.

Fast Forward to 30.

Here I am, one failed relationship after another. I am now dating Adam. It's been on and off for about eight years. I have no power in my life to say I deserve better. I wasn't empowered to say what my needs were, to walk away and stay away, or to voice what I wanted and needed in a relationship.

My life is now beyond a life of mediocrity. I am going through the motions. I was making the best of it and believing this is the best I could have. I knew that this relationship could be the one. However, I was passive, unhappy, and drank most days to hide the pain of it all.

Worst of all, I know there is more! There was more that I wanted, more that I could do, and more that I could provide for others, including Adam's four girls, who were my heart and soul. However, *knowing there was more gave me no solace.*

I knew that to make a lasting change, cause my life to shift, and live the life I could see inside; I would have to leave Adam and the girls. I knew that if I didn't leave, I'd continue living the same cycle I was stuck in, over and over. I knew I had to leave and go far, far away. Something had to change for all of our sakes. **It took leaving the country.**

That Moment Changed My Life.

My boss, Dawn, knew I was struggling, although she never said anything. She was one of the most gracious and kind women I had ever met.

It was my 30th birthday, which is one of those *significant ones.* Dawn had given me a membership to an Adventure Club, and I half-heartedly signed up for a weekend personal development course. Anything was better than what I was doing now. It led to a series of life-changing decisions, and for the first time in my life, **I was empowered.**

As the weekend drew to a close, I declared to everyone that if I could sell my car this week, I'd move to America. On Wednesday, a colleague bought my car. That was the beginning of creating a new life in America.

That same Friday, I quit my job. Two weeks later, tenants were moving into my house, and I had moved back in with my parents.

On a Plane with a Total Stranger.

Roy, my mentor from that weekend course, introduced me to a friend of his, who was living and working in Tortola in the British Virgin Islands (BVI). I was now on a plane flying to the BVI with a total stranger.

A week later, that simple decision led me to a bar on the marina waterfront. I posted a simple note on the notice board that said, "Love to see the islands." The next thing you know, I was on a private yacht, playing hostess to six millionaires, and being offered a job in Aspen, CO.

I Was Happy and Had the Dream.

Fast forward a year. It is a hot October day. I am in my future grandmother's yard, in a pretty little town in Lexington, NC, saying, **"I do."**

Now, I was happy and had the dream! Well, it didn't last long. I still wasn't empowered. Nothing had changed, except I got married. I didn't know in my heart how to empower myself.

We thought we had the dream. We thought we were going to be the couple that got everything this world promised us was possible after getting married.

It Seemed Perfect.

When I was 38, my husband's company went bankrupt. A few days later, I accepted a job at the local airport. I'd been dreaming of flying since

I was nine, and it seemed perfect. I could help the family out financially and would have fun working at the airport. The sound of the planes taking off never got old. I was living just a little sneak peek of the vision of my life that I saw on the inside and kept hoping one day I would get.

Ready for Our Move to Colorado.

Fast forward three months. The house is all packed. There are boxes everywhere, and we are ready for our road trip and our move to Colorado with our two-year-old son and the 11-week old baby in my tummy.

I am sitting at the reception desk at the airport. It's a gorgeous day outside. The pilots are happily chatting with me and checking in. I can see the planes taking off and landing through the big glass windows in front of me. I look up and see my boss walking in. He had flown down from our sister airport. He was standing in front of me with a huge smile on his face.

"Great things are coming your way, young lady!!"

I burst into tears. I hadn't said a word to my boss about my husband's company going bankrupt, nor that we were planning to move to Colorado in three days. I had kept it all to myself and had been figuring out what was next, without telling a soul.

We Moved to Colorado.

I walked away from my dream job. I would have been a pilot within the year. *I had the dream in my hands, and I walked away.* I had given my word on moving to Colorado, so we moved.

It Was Another One of Those Defining Moments.

I was sitting in the psychologist's office in California. Weeks and months of therapy all led to this moment. In one of my sessions, alone with my therapist, she said to me:

"You will love Seattle when you move there. It's an outdoor playground."

And Rachel, *"You should prepare yourself for divorce...."*

"You should buy a small house, so that you are ready to leave him."

At that moment, I had unknowingly given up on my marriage and given my word to divorce.

I Was Now Divorced, Single, With Two Kids, and Everyone's Lives Had Changed Forever.

During my divorce in 2018, I was convinced that I was leaving my husband to bring generational change to my family. I was attempting to stop reliving my mom's life. (My mom suddenly died during my divorce, and a year later, my father passed too.)

Looking back now, I can see it wasn't that at all. It was a conversation in a tiny room in California with two women, a therapist, and I, and the possibility of my marriage died.

Our Dream Died in That Moment Too.

Every action I took from there on out was not in service of my family. It was in service of getting divorced. What I was listening to, was that I was getting divorced. So, it was done.

Quite the story, right? So what's next, you might ask?

Choosing to be Empowered.

Well, standing in this life I created with all my decisions I made along the way, I am now *choosing* to be **empowered** in my life.

What changed? *Someone took a stand for my life.* Her name is Ellie Baker, and she is now one of my dearest friends. We were introduced by a mutual friend. The moment I met her, I knew she was different. She cared, in a way that I'd never experienced before. I discovered real friendship. I learned what it looked like for someone to truly listen.

There were seven whole months of almost daily walks and talks. Ellie would often say, "There's this class I took. It is just three days. I think it will make a difference for you."

Seven months later, we were having coffee in a cute little coffee shop called The Red Cup café. We were drinking our lattes in our cute red mugs, when she handed me her phone and her credit card. "Are you going to register into this class on my credit card or yours, Rachel?" And that was it. I trusted her and registered.

My Life Finally Changed for the Better.

Four short weeks later, I was in a room of about 100 people on a Friday morning in June. I discovered who I had become for myself in this journey called life. I discovered who people had become for me. I discovered being vulnerable and began learning how to share and forgive myself. I discovered real communication and found community and friendship. I discovered my voice. I discovered there was a way of listening and speaking that has everyone known, heard, seen, and understood.

What About Love?

Love is present everywhere in my life now because I say so. For right now, I'm not dating. I haven't had a single date, since I left my husband. It was by my empowered choice. I chose to be on this journey in the discovery of who I had become so that I can make a difference with my voice.

I Want Other's Lives to Be Empowered, Not Mediocre.

My life is now in service of others, finding their way to being empowered in their own lives; their families, with their children, and the teens and young adults in their lives. My goal is to have everyone living a life that's vibrant and full. **Everyone should be thriving and not just surviving.**

I discovered I became someone who took life very personally. I judged others before I was judged. I had learned to push others away to protect myself from getting hurt. I gave that up. I learned I was defending and protecting myself, by creating a life of being alone. I had created a life that matched the stories I was making up and believing in my head. It was like they were actually the truth. I am alone, not enough, terrified, not liked, rejected, discarded, ugly, fat…You know the list, right?

I am now creating a life of abundance, love, and friendship. It is messy and imperfect! I'm learning to be OK with what life looks like as we grow out of our comfort levels and into a new skin. I'm learning how to be compassionate, understanding, and joyful in communication with others. I'm learning how to not listen to the voices in my head, like they are the truth. I've learned not to make big life decisions, without talking to friends around me. They love me and empower me in all areas of my life.

With This Phase of My Life Over, Now Anything Is Possible.

There may even be romance. And it will be because an **empowered woman chose love, not a child looking to be rescued.**

What about you? Do you worry your kids might be on the same track that I was on? Maybe you don't want them or yourself to be 50, before they or you finally discover how to get free of all the stories?

Do you want to know how to empower yourself in communication, not only with your kids but with all relationships in your life? Do you want to build a Real Estate dream team? What's your dream?

Communication is key to raising a family, being an entrepreneur, running a business, and getting and being married. Whatever it is that you dream of. It is the key to everything, including having a happy and joy-filled life.

Here are my top three ways to have people be excited to be in communication with you!

1. STOP TALKING

Just for a moment, pause, take a breath, and notice what you are listening to. Not what you are saying but what you are listening to. Try it. Stop talking and listen! What are you listening to, that has you saying what you are saying?

2. GIVE IT UP

Give up being right, defending, and protecting when you are communicating. Notice that this is what we do and how most of us were trained in communication growing up. We want to make our point! Consider making a difference *not* making a point.

3. CREATE

Let go of the past. Create from nothing, with whoever you are talking to. Have them get that you hear them, *without judgement*, and watch them light up right in front of you!

Would you like to know more about being a great communicator and being empowered in your life or how you too can run the business of your dreams, create the relationship of your dreams, or live the life of your dreams? Maybe you want to empower your teens and young adults. Maybe you want to talk about Real Estate dreams and goals. I'm here to help with all of it. Reach out to me through my website or email at Empowered@RBMHomeTeam.com.

My life purpose is in being of service, and I'm waiting to hear from someone just like you to support you and your family in being empowered.

Rachel Cope

Rachel Cope is an award-winning professional Realtor, coach, and author living in Mukilteo, Washington. Originally raised in the small mining town of Bedworth, U.K., Rachel has always had big dreams, aimed high, and strived to expand her life and build her self-confidence and self-esteem. This required tough decisions, making changes, and overcoming personal adversities. Starting her professional journey at the age of 13, Rachel spent much of her early career in sales and customer service and early childhood education before switching careers to real estate. Rachel found her true self-expression as a fierce advocate for both her buyers and sellers. Whether identifying the perfect property or helping a seller make a decision to put their home on the market, Rachel's clients feel heard and cared for. Rachel is committed to communication and truly believes that it is the key to everything in life. Learning how to listen effectively is a skill that very few ever learn to truly master. She is dedicated to making sure that every family thrives with great communication skills and compassionate leadership. She lives in the State of Washington with her two children, Brandon and Mollie.

Rachel Cope
RBM Home Team
Keller Williams CPRE
22614 Bothell Everett Hwy
Bothell, WA 98021
Empowered@RBMHomeTeam.com
www.RBMHomeTeam.com

My Life Purpose Is in Being of Service to You

Want to know more about being a great communicator in your life? How you too can run the business of your dreams, create the relationship of your dreams, or if you just want to talk Real Estate dreams and goals, please reach out to me through my website.

www.RBMHomeTeam.com

Ginna Tassanelli

A Life of Hide-and-Seek Stylishly Transformed

"Trust in yourself and you will be authentic."

Remember These Words, "Ready or Not, Here I Come!"

As a child, I loved the game of hide-and-seek. It was very thrilling to hide more than to seek. When I was found, I was always ready to hide again.

Who Knew That This Game Would Be Part of My Life Story?

Is there a woman in your life that you admire and think, "Wow, she's really got it all together." "She's got an amazing husband, beautiful kids, successful business, and supportive family. How does she do it all?"

Growing up, I seemed to be the one playing by all the rules and being the good girl. Coming from a strict Catholic and Hispanic household, I definitely didn't want to let my parents down. As loving and encouraging as they've always been, not letting them down was #1 for me. At least, not letting them down in their eyes.

I had straight A's, was independent, helped as much as I could around the house, and at the age of 14, I began working part-time jobs, including working for my dad at his engineering firm doing administrative work. I was also very social, even as a little girl. So much so, I even had an imaginary friend until my brother, who's four years younger, was at an age where we could play together. I can still visualize her to this day. "Marcolina" was her name.

We have always been a very close family. We grew up loving the ocean, fishing, and traveling. Our house was never short of having parties with family and friends.

I finished college with two degrees, had a successful corporate job, got married, had kids, and was now happily ever after and on a path as a successful entrepreneur. Sounds pretty amazing. From the outside, it could seem as if I had it all together.

The thing is that for a good two decades of my life, from the age of 13 until about 33, my life was anything but "all together." During these times, my life was mostly filled with hiding. I was not hiding from others but hiding from myself, which spilled into making poor decisions that would later impact my marriage and life as a new mom.

Even though I lived in a very loving and supportive household, my life had been plagued with epidemics of distrusting myself and hiding behind all that seemed perfect.

I remember these "epidemics" beginning as I grew up dancing. I started dancing around the age of 6 through my senior year of high school. I loved dancing. It was my passion. However, it was also a passion that was not always so good for me emotionally. When I got into my teenage years, I had a completely different story in my head about my body, particularly my legs, that led me to believe I could not live up to being an elite dancer.

Looking at the other girls, in my mind, my legs were "yuck" compared to theirs. This Hispanic girl with curves and "thick" legs did not think she was good enough. I was stuck with the idea that in order to be a successful ballerina, I had to have perfectly long legs like the Sugar Plum Fairy from the Nutcracker.

I hid these feelings by hiding my legs in regular clothes. I despised wearing shorts, which was ironic because during dance, whether at practice or performing on stage, I mostly had to wear a leotard. As a beach lover, I still wore bathing suits, but if it meant wearing a garment like shorts where my legs were the main part of my body being exposed, I felt really insecure and uncomfortable.

Hiding was my way of reacting to uncomfortable challenges and was a theme that continued through my high school years, college, and even as a newbie mom.

My overall college experience is one that I'm grateful for because not only did I make life-long friendships, but that's also where I met my amazing and supportive husband. However, there were also moments between relationships, college party scenes, my own family's epidemics, and how I handled those that created more ideas of distrust within myself and hiding.

My Behaviors Were a Way of Hiding from All the Imperfections Happening in My Life Personally.

As I reached my fourth year of college and intended to continue to law school, I realized it just didn't feel right. I was really dreading continuing school, even though I had built this vision in my mind and my parents' minds of being in a courtroom putting the "bad" guys away. My mom, still to this day, says that I should have been an attorney. I think maybe my obsession with shows like Dateline got me confused about what I really wanted to do.

My decision not to continue to law school after graduation was the beginning step (so I thought) of becoming my own person. Another opportunity came right before I was getting ready to graduate, and I took it. I decided to take a corporate job as an advertising executive with the radio entertainment division at a global multi-media company.

As exciting and right as that seemed at the moment, it definitely wasn't a pivot into being my authentic self. Unfortunately, for quite some time, that seemed to be a constant in my life.

I learned a lot about the business world in a male-dominated environment within my own office and working primarily with male business owners. The novelty of working with a young woman in her 20's initially made a lot of clients willing to work with me. Looking back on it, it was not a compliment. I was lucky to work with a strong group of women that stuck together. Interestingly enough, we weren't in competition with each other, as many other "teams" with women were. Instead, we were the real definition of a team.

However, even as a top producer in my office, making six figures by the last few years of my career there, I was far from living an authentic life. I failed in many ways, with my family, and in life. I built up more distrust and disbelief within me that lead to hurting those closest to me. I made poor choices during my time there, by how I was carrying myself and putting my work ahead of my family. I was sabotaging my marriage, the respect my husband deserved, and my own self-respect.

This was my way of hiding from my messy and emotional internal conflicts that stemmed from my childhood years.

To add more fuel to the fire, other family epidemics with my immediate family were escalating that I did not know how to handle. As much as my husband tried to help the best way he knew, the more I ran.

My life was spiraling, and I needed to get a grip by taking accountability for my faults and failures to save what matters most.

The first step was to resign from my almost 10-year career and start my own advertising and marketing agency. Simultaneously, I also started a "side-hustle" as a stylist with a high-fashion jewelry company.

Are you thinking, *"Wait, you left a successful career that was taking over your life, to start your own business and a side-hustle, and you're trying not to put your work first and work as much?"*

Well, sort of. I made the leap so that I could have control over my life and be the wife and mother I've always wanted to be and that my family deserved while seeking a personal and professional life of intention and purpose.

It's what needed to happen for me to realize that succeeding was really coming face to face with my faults and failures in order to pursue a purposeful life. It wasn't about how much money I was making or how well I could hide from my failures.

This realization did not happen as soon as I turned in my resignation.

The intent was there, but it still took another few years to really be honest with myself and accept my failures without letting them define me.

In a perfect world, my failures would not exist, or I would have made the decision to have faced them much sooner. However, I did not trust myself and hid behind my fear that took control.

In the Real World, My Failures Will Not Define Me.

As I worked through my fears of being authentic in my personal life and life as a "mom-preneur" became more normal, my businesses began to flourish. However, there was still something missing that was holding me back from succeeding as an entrepreneur — ME.

I Was Still Hiding. This Time I Was Hiding Behind My Business.

When I resigned from my corporate job, I was fortunate to start my agency with a handful of clients. However, after a few years, I felt like I hit a wall. I wasn't scaling, and even though I thought I was doing all the things — I had my logo, website, services, referrals, networking, the business wasn't moving in the direction I had hoped for by this time.

I began to network locally and remembered seeing and hearing a consistent pattern from other entrepreneurs when they would stand up and give their one-minute "elevator pitches." Many elevator pitches (including mine) did not sound confident and instead lead with their services or products without really communicating what problems their products or services solved.

I realized then that as entrepreneurs trying to market ourselves online, although our genuine intent is seeking to provide solutions for our ideal clients, many of us also hide behind our business by trying to sell our products and services, instead of showing up as our unique selves to make human connections that serve and influence. That is exactly what I was doing and why I was hitting a wall.

Coming from a corporate advertising background, I was used to helping small to medium-sized businesses and national brands market their business brand locally. This meant marketing through traditional medias, so that they could increase their brand recognition and ROI on advertising initiatives. There wasn't a real human connection between their ideal customer and the owner of the business brand. My time at my corporate job was also before social media even existed, and it ended right at the beginning when some of the platforms were invented.

It Finally Hit Me!

What was missing from my business was a foundational step that I completely skipped over! I was not showing up as myself within my business. I acted as if I had the right to show up as a little unknown business brand in a world of BIG business brands. So, I started to change how I was showing up. I began to lead with me. There was no more hiding.

As an agency, I continued to help my done-for-you clients market themselves as the business brand that they are. However, for me, personally, moving forward, I started to learn how to develop my personal brand, which meant I needed to stop hiding and start showing up as myself.

Showing up as a personal brand meant that I had to connect my values, my experiences, my story, and myself with my business in a way that added a human effect to my business so that my ideal clients could get to know and trust me.

Once I became aware of this, the next obstacle to overcome was, "Why me? Who am I to inspire other human beings as a Personal Brand? Why should I have any authority in this space?"

This is just a mindset game I was playing with myself.

I'm sure you've heard the phrase *"imposter syndrome."* It was creeping up on me fast!

So, instead of avoiding actions, I was taking actions. If I were to be rejected, that was okay. Rejection just meant they weren't my people, and I had room for the right people to support. I also stopped justifying what I charge.

The more I practiced all of this, the more I began being the one sought after by the right types of clients, support systems, and communities that aligned with my purpose and values.

As time went on, my confidence grew. I became more aware that my failures would not define me. I was able to shut down those imposter thoughts (most of the time…I am human, and they still creep up from time to time) and continue to take action, rather than just sitting on the backside of my business. I knew that I had to show up, even if it was imperfectly, so that I could be my authentic self because I am imperfect.

I needed to use the online tools available to us (social media and digital platforms) with intent as a vehicle to get my personal brand out there, deliver value and create authority in my space.

Taking action looked like this — stepping out of my comfort zone and focusing on my ideal clients, not on me. This meant showing up with value by providing solutions to my ideal clients' challenges instead of pushing my products or services.

As entrepreneurs, our products and services are the promise we make to providing solutions, but to get to that point, our ideal clients must first trust us. Therefore, just plastering my logo and website all over the place was not enough.

When we are marketing ourselves online, it's necessary to provide value in order to earn people's trust. As much as we'd like for people to just open their wallet and throw their credit card at us because they've seen our logo or website, it just doesn't happen that way. It takes time to build that trust.

Some of the ways I did that and continue to do so today, are by offering complimentary social media content reviews and audits, hosting live streaming sessions discussing topics that my ideal clients ask about, engaging and communicating within my community and others, collaborating with other experts, speaking engagements, and investing in support.

Throughout this process of developing my personal brand, I began experiencing a more personal transformation. Not only did my business evolve, but the personal growth I was experiencing, together with my "side-hustle" as a stylist, was coming full circle. I began loving myself more and accepting my body. With honesty came the acceptance that my failures do not define me. I also felt empowered and confident in my own skin, curves, and all.

The more empowered I felt, the more consistently I was showing up in my business, and the more passionate I became in sharing this experience with other female entrepreneurs. My work as a stylist shifted to image consulting, teaching women how to rediscover their own style because I realized that style was more than looking good. Rediscovering one's personal style and aligning it with our personal brand was a way to increase confidence and a way to express myself and my personal brand more authentically.

When one's personal style and personal brand do not align, the process feels awkward and influences our level of confidence. My lack of belief in myself was because I lacked my own confidence. For me, that goes all the way back to my adolescent days as a dancer. We are influenced by the way we feel about how we look.

Although style is what we clothe our body with, which deals with the external, it is actually deeply internal. What we wear is a visual expression of our self-perception. If we are not comfortable with our style or think we have no style, we are probably not comfortable with our body image. The work begins with accepting our unique body and learning how to dress for it in a way that aligns with a style that expresses our very best self no matter our size, weight, or shape.

I've recognized that the choices we make in the way we present and express ourselves have a direct effect on how we understand and honor our inner drive. In my experience, too many women hide. They are reluctant to express themselves visually through their personal style and other lifestyle choices for fear of upsetting someone or being branded a 'show-off'. However, expressing yourself visually through your personal style and aligning that with your personal brand is extremely enriching and empowering.

Taking bolder steps when you make a bolder style choice that feels authentic can translate to taking bolder steps in business, money, and family life. A bold style is something I recognized through my mom's personal style. She is the first "fashion queen" in my life that taught me the importance of getting dressed no matter the occasion.

There is a perception that how we dress is insignificant in the grand scheme of things. I've met and mentored many women that also directly or subconsciously do not wish to be seen. Therefore, they don't understand the internal impact their personal style can do for them.

Our style, whether we want it to or not, can have a negative or positive effect on our mood and behavior. When we wear clothes we like and feel fabulous in, we show up with confidence to the world. This confidence we experience directly influences our feeling of self-worth.

For many years, my self-esteem suffered because I did not know who I was and how I wanted to show up. I was so focused on hiding. It is hard to convince others about one's abilities and skills if we don't know who we are.

Making a conscious decision to become braver requires intention. Sometimes we need a small push from the universe, or in my case, a BIG push (realizing that money doesn't equal success) for a life-changing experience. I realized that I couldn't hide from myself. I had to start taking control of my identity.

Although progress to finding my identity may not have been rapid, drifting through life without challenging myself, trying new things, or continuing to grow would mean staying stuck in an ugly place of hiding.

When you start dealing with your faults, failures, challenges and pushing yourself, you will find that your confidence grows. You become comfortable pushing yourself out of your comfort zone. With more confidence and more action on your goals, you begin to realize your true potential.

As a wife, mom, and entrepreneur of two successful businesses that align with who I am today, I now seek new positive challenges and opportunities and live a life of intention and purpose so that I can inspire other high-achieving women to do the same and live their calling.

My goal, regardless of whether it has been through jewelry and fashion accessory sales or personal styling and image consulting through The Style Rebel Mama, or social media marketing strategies and consulting through HYPE Media, Inc., has always been to help women achieve their goals and dreams by *Stylishly Branding* the best version of themselves with authenticity.

This is the legacy I want to leave behind to my children so that they understand that their faults and failures are not what defines them. We all have them, and we all have a story. What matters is how you can use your story to positively impact others.

We also all have the choice to re-write our story through one that is filled with humbleness, honesty, self-love, kindness, and inspiration.

"When you choose to seek an authentic life instead of hiding from it, you will know who you are meant to be and how you can make an impact."
—Ginna Tassanelli

That is one of the most powerful lessons I have learned throughout my journey.

Ginna Tassanelli

When Ginna Tassanelli realized the power of self-love, confidence, and facing challenges, she realized that life is full of incredible opportunities when you seek them instead of hiding from them. As a wife and "mom-preneur," Ginna knows what it's like to juggle the day-to-day while seeking a life of intention and purpose with authenticity. She was born in San Juan, Puerto Rico, and moved to the United States when she was three years old. Ginna grew up in the entrepreneurial world watching her Dad run his engineering firms. After graduating from Florida State University in 2000 with a bachelor's degree in both Criminology and Communication Studies, she began a career as an advertising executive with a leading global multi-media company for nine years. In 2009, she decided it was time to seek her own entrepreneurial journey by simultaneously launching HYPE Media, Inc., a boutique social media marketing agency, and the Style Rebel Mama, as an image consultant and personal stylist. These two brands have evolved into Stylishly Branding with Ginna. HYPE Media, Inc. continues to support businesses with social media marketing, paid traffic strategies, and consulting services. Ginna and her team have worked with dozens of businesses in the restaurant, mortgage, nightclub, interior design, e-commerce, and B2B industries, just to name a few. In 2019, Ginna's time mentoring and consulting with clients inspired her to bring her passion and expertise in marketing strategies, image consulting, and personal branding together to support female entrepreneurs by Stylishly Branding through her mentorship programs. It provided them with the tools to build and grow their own influence, personal brand, and business. Whether through personal styling or personal brand development and social media marketing strategies, Ginna's mission is to help women achieve their goals and dreams of making a bigger impact by being the best version of themselves.

Ginna Tassanelli
Stylishly Branding
6574 N. State Road 7, #155
Coconut Creek, FL 33073
561-386-0958
Ginna@StylishlyBranding.com
www.StylishlyBranding.com

Personal Brand, Style, and Visibility Guide

In this guide, you discover the step-by-step foundations to building an intentional and magnetic personal brand that aligns with you and your perfect audience so that you can attract, inspire, and make a bigger impact in their lives and yours.

www.StylishlyBranding.com/brandvisibilityguide

Cathy Compton

It's About the People, the Leadership, and the Journey

As a kid, I would often lay in my beanbag chair, in the damp basement of my upstate NY home, listening to music and dream of one day becoming someone special. I wanted to do something extraordinary that nobody else had done. I would visualize myself being carried off the field and waking up the next day with my name on the front page of the local newspaper. I knew at a very early age that I was destined to be successful and I was ready for the ride, or so I thought. I loved sports and was very athletic, the epitome of a "Tomboy." That vision of doing something special and being the best played over and over again in my mind. It stayed with me well into my adult life as a college athlete and eventually a college and professional softball coach. That vision would eventually become a reality.

The Climb

I went to college right out of high school and majored in sports, occasionally spending time going to classes and studying when I had to. By my senior year, I knew that my dream to be the best in the world would not be fulfilled as an athlete, so I did the next best thing and became a coach. I started my coaching career at a tiny school in Illinois called Eureka College. Fresh out of grad school, I discovered that I had a unique ability to take ordinary, average kids and mold them into champions and championship teams. These young athletes played for the love of the game and left everything they had on the field. Five years later, I jumped at the chance to coach NCAA Division 1 softball at Nichols State and eventually landed at LSU. I had made it to the "Big Leagues." Now came the hard part. I had to win and win often.

All About the WIN

Coaching big-time scholarship athletes was a whole different ballgame. I often missed my scrappy team from the Midwest. I did what many coaches do in the sports world and I dedicated my life to pursuing the WIN. Tireless hours on the field, driving for days in a van, shuffling kids from hotel to hotel, and eventually, the hard work and commitment paid off. It was the beginning of a long and successful coaching career. The more we won, the more I had to win. It eventually became more of an obsession than a career. I had convinced myself that was how it was done. It was the road one had to take to make it to the top, win it all, and fulfill the ultimate goal. I was driven to be the best, to win, and was certain that winning would eventually make me happy. Unfortunately, the wins were short-lived, and the losses, while few and far between, were agonizing. I just kept going; after all, what could be better than my name in the record books and having Nike pay me thousands of dollars to wear the swoosh?

The next chapter of my coaching career began with a long drive over Lake Pontchartrain into Louisiana. I had built championship teams and had won at smaller schools, so I knew it was possible to win with talented, elite athletes. Just as I had planned, we won from the beginning and never looked back. I had seen it so vividly as a kid sitting in my basement. The dream to be the best, win it all, and have my picture hung in a Hall of Fame was about to become real. My life would never be the same.

The Miracle That Changed It All

We were having one of those magical seasons, the ones they make movies about. We were nearing the end of our season. Our team was leading the conference and on a winning streak. Schools were starting to recruit me to coach for them and offering me big money. The team was on a roll and clicking on all cylinders. We were about to play a team that was way out of our league. The worst part, we would have to travel from Louisiana thousands of miles in a van packed with kids and luggage to play an undefeated USC team that was on a 34 home game winning streak. I had mentally prepared the "we did the best we could" speech and gave the team a day to decompress at the beach. The USC team we were playing was the equivalent of the 1980 Soviet Union Olympic ice hockey team. They were UNBEATABLE, and they knew it!!! When we pulled up in our school van, we could hear some of the fans laughing, and the sports information director make a "not so funny" joke as we rolled out of the van. My 4'10" center fielder leaned over and said, "Coach, they are twice our size, remind us again. Why are we here?" I laughed and said, "Listen, we came all this way to play ball, and that's what we are going to do." I had made a career of taking unrecruited, average underdog athletes and teaching them how to win. As any great coach would do, I had prepared and actually convinced them that they would win. After all, we were expected to lose. The odds were so heavily stacked against us that technically, we should not even get a single hit off of their pitcher, let alone score a run or win the game.

Well, the rest is history. Not only did we score a run, we scored three runs, and the kid who got the game-winning hit had grown up in that town. It turns out they said she was not "good enough" to play for them. We all held our breath as the last out was made. The game was over, and WE HAD WON. The crowd was stunned, and you could hear a pin drop in the stadium. That was until my team came screaming out of the dugout and nearly tackled our pitcher. The local kids were lining up along the fence with their game program and pens in hand, ready to get our autographs. The moment was surreal. A vision I had dreamed about as a kid hundreds of times had become a reality. I could see the scoreboard flashing the score and the puzzled look on the thousand plus fans, who were shocked and stunned at what had just happened. The parents who had driven cross country to see us play were hugging everyone in sight and crying hysterically, as my team ran out onto the field to celebrate the victory. We had just done the imaginable. We had just beaten an "unbeatable team" on their home field. It was a modern-day version of the 1980 Olympic miracle on ice.

It played out exactly how I had seen it over and over again in my mind and in my dreams as a kid. It was a surreal experience that was real yet seemed like a dream. Interestingly, my feet felt like cement, and everything around me slowed down as if it was in slow motion. It was as if I was frozen in time and in place. My players and the dozen loyal parents and fans who made the trip with us were jumping up and down and hugging each other. Tears were streaming down the faces of many of the players on the team. The energy was electrifying, yet I somehow could not feel it. The moment I had waited for my entire life had just happened, and my body felt numb. I remembered whispering to myself, "This can't be it.... Is this really it?" It was the moment that I had spent my entire life and coaching career preparing for—that breathtaking moment when you take the last step and reach the top of the summit. Only to find that the view is no different from the top, not at all what you were expecting. We had just had our own "miracle on ice" moment. Yet, I was left with this indescribable, empty, unfulfilled feeling. Thousands of shocked fans surrounded us, TV cameras capturing every move, and athletes running around like little kids, yet I was numb to the experience.

The Start of the End

We somehow made it back to Louisiana, only to find that we had made it on the front page of USA Today with an article titled "David Beat Goliath." Our campus was buzzing with excitement, and everyone wanted to hear the story. I was getting calls from famous people I didn't even know. I will never forget that moment where history was made. My players talked about and shared the experience with their own kids for years. That was a pivotal, turning point in my life when I began to discover that maybe, just maybe, the game of softball... and the game of life.... was not about the score. I could not be with the thought that maybe my journey to the top, my success, and my legacy was not defined by the number of wins, and there were more than 400 of them. It was a coaching record that brought me big-time endorsements, coach of the year awards, and a seat in two Halls of Fame. 25+ years later, some of the NCAA records we had set have still not been broken. In that magical moment, I had discovered something most coaches spend a lifetime searching for, the secret to success. The bigger surprise was that the success did not feel any different. It took me days to settle down and to realize I had been focusing on the wrong things. Success was not about the talent, the records broken, the awards, or the Hall of Fame plaques. At the highlight of my career, I discovered it was not about reaching the summit. It was actually about **the JOURNEY** and the climb to the summit. I was so busy winning; I forgot to experience the experience of it all. It wasn't about the accolades, awards, or even the lucrative checks from Nike. It was about **the LEADERS** who were born and the difference they would go on to make in the world. Some of them became leaders of major corporations. Above all else, it was about **the PEOPLE** (the team) and the bond that was created, and who they got to be. It was a once-in-a-lifetime moment that only a championship team gets to experience when the sum of the parts becomes greater than the whole. I had uncovered the ultimate secret that **TEAM** actually meant:

Together

Everyone

Achieves

More

Furthermore, every sports team, company, and group could have that experience, and I was the one to provide it.

It's About the People (the Team)

Having discovered the secret to success, I set out on a mission to share it with anyone who would listen. Most were fascinated with how I had won so many games with so little talent. Even Pete Rose reminded me that I had made it into the Hall of Fame. A goal he had not yet accomplished. As fate would have it, I met an extraordinary man thru mutual friends. They added we were like "2 peas in a pod" and insisted that I could make a difference for him. The moment he began to share, I was inspired. I had never met nor worked with someone so integral, so accomplished, and yet so humble. I will never forget the night Alex shared his story with me. I recall promising him that they would make a movie of his life one day, and his books would become as popular as Victor Frankel's *Man's Search for Meaning*. Alex had also dreamed of accomplishing great things as a kid. He fulfilled that dream by making it to the Olympics as a German wrestler. He poured out every detail of his experience and openly shared his life with me.

The year was 1980, and the Olympics had ended. Alex and the team flew back to Germany for a red carpet celebration. It was the beginning of a nightmare that would become the worst day of his life. As Alex stepped foot on the red carpet, he was met by two armed police officers, who quickly lead him away. They cuffed him and put him in prison, charging him with being a political prisoner for a comment he made about the boycott of the Olympics. At first, he was convinced it was a mistake until they showed him the newspaper article with his quote. It turned out that the guy he chatted with was a newspaper reporter. Alex spent the next several years being beaten, starved, and tortured. Guards ridiculed him for ending up in prison for merely making a comment. Eventually, they offered to let him go free if he would simply say that the reporter made up the story. Alex refused the offer to lie in exchange for freedom. I struggled to comprehend the gruesome details of the torture Alex endured. It was worse than any horror story I had ever read or seen on TV. The story then took a turn.

One day while lying on his cement bed, contemplating giving up the fight to live, Alex watched a team of ants crawling across the bedpost carrying a crumb from the stale bread they fed the prisoners. He watched how the ants all worked together in unison, achieving something as a team that they could not do on their own—each one committedly doing its part. Somewhat delirious, Alex found comfort in the ants working together and experiencing teamwork. It was just enough of a distraction from his reality to give him hope that one day he could eventually leave his prison cell and create a new life. Months later, they gave Alex a shirt and pants and pushed him over the East Germany border, telling him that he would never survive and to never return to his country.

Never Underestimate the Heart of a Champion

They say what doesn't kill you makes you stronger. Alex's prison experience had an enormous impact on him. As he shared more and more, we began to create the next chapter of his life. While dealing with unbearable circumstances, he had discovered the power of teamwork and his passion for people. Alex made his way to the US, built a successful real estate business, became a world champion in Jiu-Jitsu, married, had kids, and the rest is history. Together, we uncovered his passion for coaching people and started an international coaching business empowering people. It was never about the medals, the awards, or even the torture. It was about **the TEAM and the "PEOPLE."**

Focus on the Leadership

As a Hall of Fame coach, I discovered championship teams and successful companies had something in common. Both were the result of focusing on the people, not the wins or widgets. I had also proven it was the leaders who made the biggest impact on the team's success. If strong leadership produced record-breaking results with softball teams, I was certain it would do the same with companies and organizations. A few years ago, I was introduced to some players on a pro baseball team that was struggling to win games. They were in last place in their division. I don't have permission to use their name, so I will call them "A-TEAM." They clearly had the talent, yet they were underperforming as a team. I took a risk and had a straight, unapologetic conversation and provided coaching that would have a significant impact on the team and their performance. In a conversation with one of the best players in the league, I coached him on what was missing and what it would take to turn the team around. I told him that the team would win when he provided leadership. Without leadership, they would continue to lose. Given my credentials and coaching record, he took my word for it. "G" was a great athlete and hard worker who was well respected as a quiet, humble team player. In our conversation, "G" discovered that it wasn't enough that he lead by example. He needed to be vocal and be willing to challenge the team to level up.

I will never forget the call I received from one of the trainers near the end of the season, who shared the difference that coaching had made on "G." The team had climbed from last place to first place and was one game away from the World Series. They lost that final game, thus ending the comeback season of the century. "G" had unleashed his leadership and had his best season, finishing just a few votes shy of the MVP in his division. "G's" leadership made the difference in the team's performance. *Successful teams and companies develop strong leaders, and strong leaders lead to successful results.* Sports teams are no different than companies or countries, for that matter. Leadership is the critical element that pulls it all together.

I love the movie *The Wizard of Oz* and the analogies to life and leadership. There are twists and turns, flying monkeys, and even munchkin fans. There are dead-end roads that lead to nowhere. When you peel back the curtain of the great Oz, you discover some dude pushing buttons and pulling levers pretending to be mighty and powerful. In the end, the real power was there all along (in the Ruby Red shoes). That power is available to everyone. All it takes is the willingness to step into the shoes and do the work to develop the leader within. The results will follow.

It's All About the Journey — Making a Difference

How fitting that I ended my softball coaching career coaching the Durham Dragons, a professional softball team televised on ESPN at the once-famous "Bull Durham" field. The end of the journey is just the beginning of the next journey. Sixteen years of coaching championship teams and I was just starting to connect the dots.

Then I met an extraordinary man named Jonathan, who was one of the most fascinating, talented, and passionate human beings I had ever met. Jonathan was no ordinary Joe. He was a licensed yacht master, having captained over 35,000 nautical miles around the world. He was a free-diver of 100 feet with one breath, a master scuba diver with ascents of Mount Rainier and Mount Sinai, and he had traveled and lived in over 30 countries. Jonathan was an inventor and designer of advanced surgical instruments that helped saved lives. However, it was a story he shared with me about what he discovered while living in a van in the outback of Australia in the middle of nowhere that touched, moved, and inspired me beyond words and would be the start of a remarkable partnership.

Jonathan had set out on a journey in the Outback to "Find Himself." That path would take him miles away from civilization, living in a van by himself and surviving on limited food and water. He had reached a point where he had to make a decision to bathe himself or use the remaining water supply to stay hydrated. Much like Alex, there was a pivotal moment where something unpredictable happened that would alter everything. He came up with an idea that would be a game-changer for a problem that most were turning a blind eye to, and few were willing to address. It was in this delirious, stressful moment in the van that Jonathan came up with an idea that would solve an age-old issue with regard to water. This idea would become his life's purpose and his mission. There were 2.3 billion people currently living in highly water-stressed situations, and cities around the world facing their "Day Zero" when they run out of tap water and must begin importing freshwater simply to survive. There are also 140 million people who are drinking contaminated water. Yes, water is a real-world issue that, up until now, was not being addressed.

Staring at the last of his water supply, Jonathan began to write down notes on how to get the most out of every drop of water. That would lead to an invention that would alter the way we use water and the creation of a cutting-edge company called Geyser Technologies. The prototype was successfully launched and raised the necessary investment money to take this product to the world. They say, "You can't stop an idea whose time has come." This device is already available in specialty stores and is saving an estimated 18 million gallons of water in 2021. We created a dream team and a plan to make a difference that will impact water issues around the world.

My coaching career had gone full circle and ended right where I started, with a dream to do something extraordinary and make an impact. The new game is to give away what I discovered about success, team and teamwork and develop future leaders. Each of us are given a limited time here on earth, and we get to choose how we spend that time and where we focus our attention. As a softball coach, I reached the top of the summit, only to discover that who I always wanted to be, was not who I really was. What I thought was so important, was not really important at all. Life was not just about winning. In the end, what really matters is the difference that is made. Every team, company, and organization can become a high-performing team and produce unprecedented results. Focusing on the people, the leadership, and the journey is the secret to success.

Cathy Compton

For over 20 years, Cathy Compton has been coaching and training championship teams and empowering leaders, companies, and organizations. With an extensive background in coaching world-class athletes, she has coached, trained, and/or consulted top-level CEO's, corporate executives, olympic athletes, business owners, Major League Baseball, and leaders committed to high-level performance. She is passionate that people discover their power and move beyond their limits to live a created and fulfilling life. As a peak performance coach, Cathy ranks as one of the most successful college coaches in NCAA Softball and is a member of two college Halls of Fame. Her expertise is in the area of building teams and teamwork within organizations, developing leadership and communication skills, and impacting the world of performance. As a certified and licensed trainer and coach for Codebreaker Technologies, Cathy trains companies and individuals to enhance their communication skills within the team, recruit and retain the best and increase sales. As a certified facilitator for the Extreme Leadership Institute, Cathy teaches the Extreme Leadership methods proven to create radical results for individuals and organizations. Power, performance, and a deep-rooted commitment to bringing out the best in human beings earned Cathy the prestigious ICON award with Codebreaker Technologies in 2020. As Abraham Lincoln said, "Our tomorrows need new and different solutions today." The time is now to discover leadership and level up. Winning is about the people, the leadership, and the journey.

Cathy Compton
2231 E. Karen Drive
Phoenix, AZ 85022
480-292-5322
id8coach@gmail.com
www.LinkedIn.com/in/Cathy-Compton-5398641

Crack Your Personality BANK Code

Discover the secret, the science, and the system that gives you access to extraordinary relationships, unprecedented sales results, and the opportunity to make a real difference!

Crack your code to receive a free report. ($97 Value)

Crackmycode.com/Leadership

Dr. Marilu Almeida Hunt

Rest and Digest to Feel Your Best

The origin of my digestive health journey began with a shocking and profound proclamation. ***"Recent studies show that today's generation of children may have a shorter life expectancy than their parents!"*** resonated across the auditorium of the medical conference. This shocking statement made me immediately concerned for my children's health. From that moment on, I was inspired to understand the keys to true physical health. My journey is the culmination of years of education, personal digestive experience, and ultimately my endeavor to educate and better the gut health of others.

My name is Marilu Almeida Hunt, Pharm.D., CPh, CIHC, INHC, the founder of Gut Recharge, LLC. My goal is to help educate and socialize the complex nature of the human body's digestive system and translate the language the body uses to scream dysfunction. The "Gut," aka "gastrointestinal tract," is not only our body's most under-appreciated organ, but it's also the brain's most important advisor.

Digestion Is an Issue That Is Central to Our Health.

We are currently living in an unprecedented environment with COVID-19. This pandemic has exposed the health risks arising from a compromised immune system. Astonishingly, the digestive system, our microbiome, houses 70% of our immune system. The body's immune system depends on bacteria in the gut to determine what is a foreign invader, toxin, or pathogen.

The Gut Is a Crucial Gatekeeper That Protects Our Insides from the Outside World.

Growing up, I constantly struggled with digestive issues. My parents, both immigrants from Cuba, would offer me homeland remedies for my digestive ailments. I remember insisting that these remedies weren't helping. However, they claimed: "In Cuba, these always help." I remember thinking to myself, "But Mom, we're not in Cuba. We're in America."

My health issues were not a simple matter of a child eating junk food coupled with a lack of exercise. I was a star, three-sport athlete in high school who was often featured in the local paper. I even received a small profile in Sports Illustrated. I was excelling in both sports and academics, yet dealing with constant stomach pain, indigestion, bloating, and heartburn.

"She was unstoppable, not because she didn't have failures or doubts, but because she continued on despite them."

—Beau Taplin

After high school, I attended the University of Notre Dame and played on the school's softball team. Following my undergraduate studies, I earned a Doctor of Pharmacy (Pharm.D.) degree at Mercer University, Southern School of Pharmacy. During this time, my symptoms worsened, and I finally went to see a gastroenterologist. The doctor ordered a gamut of testing and prescribed various medications. Some medications helped me marginally, others not at all. After these successive failures, I came to accept that I would be battling with these symptoms for the rest of my life.

With my degree, I became a clinical pharmacist at a hospital. This is quite different from working at your local drug store. In a hospital, clinical pharmacists work directly with doctors to monitor inpatient care. Patients arrive at hospitals in their sickest states. Working with the medical staff, clinical pharmacists are responsible for organizing and adjusting patients' medication regimens. Over time, I noticed a consistent problem. The same patients kept returning. I frequently wondered **why?** Perhaps we were only responding to the surface-level problem and not addressing the underlying systemic issue. **What was the real root cause of their symptoms?**

Shortly after this revelation, the pace of my life rapidly accelerated. I became a wife, a Mom, and raised three children while still balancing my professional career. At the hospital, I was promoted to the Director of Pharmacy Services, which was an extremely demanding position. I loved my job, but the stress levels were very high! In addition to more responsibilities, I was also teaching pharmacy students as an adjunct pharmacy professor for three different universities.

Tangent to the evolution and progression of my life, my digestive health continued to deteriorate. When my hands began to swell, and I felt pain in my joints, I became alarmed. As a mother and busy professional, I needed to find a solution to improve my health. My doctors speculated that I might have an auto-immune disease. I later learned that when the gut is not working properly, unexpected symptoms can appear. These symptoms include typical gut and abdominal symptoms, but also other seemingly unrelated symptoms, such as inflammation and joint pain. I had a **leaky gut (aka "intestinal permeability").** This involves tiny "leaks" in our gut lining that can allow unnecessary, potentially toxic molecules (besides nutrients and water) into our bodies' circulation. For more information on leaky gut, visit https://gutrecharge.com/understanding-leaky-gut/.

It began to dawn on me that we all shop at grocery stores that are teeming with thousands of items, many of which are processed and attractively packaged. Profit-driven companies, "Big Food," want to extend shelf life, making claims that their food is "healthy." However, the average consumer doesn't realize that these foods are saturated with sugar, fat, and artificial preservatives. We refer to these foods as part of the **SAD (Standard American Diet)**, which only leads to disease. We are being described as the fast-food generation, allowing our busy lives to lead us to simple, easy options, like fast-food restaurants with inexpensive, oversized value meals.

Undoubtedly, there is a clear and important role for medication in healthcare. Unfortunately, **medications are often being prescribed as "band-aids"** that only mask problems without actually curing them. Big Pharma is constantly advertising that medication is the answer, but is it? I concluded that the healthcare system is too focused on disease state management rather than complete health.

Sick-Care Versus Healthcare?

Frustrated, I began to focus my attention on **disease state prevention and health promotion.** I started listening to my own body, dove into research solutions, and took a closer look at my gut health.

Unexpectedly, my life took another sudden turn. My husband was given an incredible new professional opportunity that prompted a move to Geneva, Switzerland. This sudden transition to a new lifestyle and culture offered me new perspectives that would forever alter my wellness journey.

Upon first arriving in Geneva, I mistakenly thought that our new way of life had begun to regress. It has always been ingrained in me that our most valuable resources are time and money. However, surrounded by a new perspective, I gained an appreciation that **true wealth was measured in one's health.** We learned to slow down rather than rush through life. The trite phrase "Europeans work to live while Americans live to work" truly presented itself and rang true.

Hippocrates once philosophized,

> *"Let food be thy medicine and medicine be thy food."*

> *"All disease begins in the gut."*

The **"AHA"** moment!

Throughout my life, I enjoyed attending educational conferences and meetings on a wide range of medical topics. During my time in Switzerland, I attended a conference on "Integrative Nutrition and Gut Health" that expanded my perspective and changed my life. It provided a clarity that aligned all of my past experiences and discoveries around the imperativeness and importance of the gut.

My shift in strategy was propelled by a renewed understanding of functional medicine, integrative nutrition, and the gut. The function of the digestive system fascinated me. I began cleaning up my diet so that my gut could *"stop leaking"* and start healing. I sought out quality probiotics, vitamins, and minerals that helped me heal. I began taking foundational supplements that help reduce chronic inflammation and protect my body from diseases. Slowly but certainly, I began to feel better.

Health Doesn't Happen Overnight!

It takes time to start digesting foods and having normal regular bowel movements. After a few weeks, my swelling vanished. I saw first-hand the powerful impact of my new regimen. I was able to enjoy eating again, focus on work, play with my kids, and sleep all night! I opened a can of tennis balls for the first time in months and began holding my tennis racket. The changes I made had a wealth of benefits. I was hooked.

Success in treating my health problems inspired me to pass my knowledge to others. I started with my family. We all began to cook healthy, clean meals, dining regularly together as a family. Since foods today aren't as nutrient-dense as they used to be, everyone began taking vitamins and supplements. We exercised regularly, started deep breathing exercises and yoga! Our battles with digestive health receded and disappeared. My eldest daughter graduated from college early with her master's degree and is now loving law school. My middle daughter is thriving in her undergraduate experience and applying to medical school. My son is a Division I collegiate swimmer and excelling academically.

After realizing a fork and knife may be the most powerful tool to transform our health, I decided to turn my passion into a consulting business: Gut Recharge, LLC. Whether you eat meals at home, work, or school, **every meal should be considered an essential part of a healthy lifestyle.**

No Matter How Fast You Run, You Can't Outrun the SAD Diet.

"Gold medals aren't really made of gold. They're made of sweat,
determination, and a hard-to-find alloy called guts!"

—Dan Gable

I started working with athletes of all ages. These athletes were stuck in a similar cycle of going to doctors seeking help but finding no respite. One of my clients came to me with gut problems that were inhibiting her ability to thrive in her sport. Frustrated, she reached out to me, hoping to learn more about gut health and to find new ways to improve her nutrition, performance, and happiness. My client was suffering from stomach aches, bloating, and constipation. A determined, disciplined student-athlete dedicated to her sport and academics, she was ready to make changes. We reviewed her diet strategy, began focusing on what she felt like after she ate her meals and snacks, and started adding simple healthy foods that we called a "performance plate." I then started removing foods that seemed problematic, added some supplements that helped her gut digest and absorb nutrients. Before long, she started having regular bowel movements, which she called a "miracle." Not only did she start to feel "human" again, but she began to excel on the field. Her coaches noticed and moved her up to the varsity squad!

Athletes Need Efficient Fuel That Gets Them to the Finish Line.

I realize that athletes typically don't know what to eat or when to eat. The timing of meals is critical during training and especially before competitions. Athletes can't afford to have stomach aches or cramps in the middle of their events. They don't have time to run off to the bathroom during competitions. They can't be sick from crazy training schedules when it's time to compete.

My Mission Was Never Clearer.

It was to educate athletes regarding gut health and balanced, targeted nutrition. This precision approach empowers and supports their journey to optimal performance. I enjoy teaching athletes how to listen to their bodies, properly assess body aches and cravings, and how to feed their body what it needs to repair itself.

My method is simple, effective, and sustainable:

1. Audit your diet, environment, stressors, and exercise program.

2. Remove what is bad, toxic, or harmful.

3. Add back what is good, healthy, and mindful at the appropriate time.

4. Recharge and restore a healthy balance.

80/20 Rule: 80% Focused + 20% Fun = 100% Effective.

Reflecting back to my childhood days, I was fortunate to have the wisdom of my Cuban medical parents, my father a physician, and my mother a pharmacist, who believed in the value of pharmaceuticals but also taught us to look outside the box for holistic healing options such as nutraceuticals. I learned that the body has remarkable healing power. We need to support and empower our bodies by restoring our inner balance. It's overwhelming how many probiotics and other supplements are available today. The number of different combinations available at health food stores is growing rapidly.

This is where my **expertise matters.** Working with an educated, integrative, functional, gut health specialist (Gut Recharge, LLC) who can recommend quality products can make the journey more focused, fun, and effective.

It's OK to Not Be Perfect 20% of the Time and Have Fun!

By 2030, it is predicted that 50% of the population will have some form of chronic disease. Unfortunately, there is no *"magic pill"* to fix their problems. People are busy and don't have time to research medications, nutritional supplements, and other remedies. Athletes are unique because their needs are diverse yet specific. Their bodies must perform at their optimum level at exactly the right time.

Train Longer?

I say, **"train smarter."** Recover faster and become more focused. Feel stronger. Most importantly, **improve to win, not just at sports, but at life-because without health, you can't stay in the game.**

"In any moment of decision, the best thing you can do is the right thing,
the next best thing you can do is the wrong thing, and the worst thing
you can do is nothing."

—Theodore Roosevelt

Dr. Marilu Almeida Hunt

Dr. Marilu Almeida Hunt is a Certified International Health Coach and Functional Medicine Pharmacist. She worked for 17 years at University Hospital in South Florida as a Clinical Pharmacist and the Director of Pharmacy Services. She also served as an adjunct clinical professor during her tenure. She specialized in disease state management and was a national speaker for several major pharmaceutical companies.

After years of working in the hospital, Dr. Hunt realized she needed to move in a new direction. Therefore, she began to focus on Integrative Nutrition and Functional Medicine. She earned her Integrative Nutrition Health Coach certification from the Institute of Integrative Nutrition and is an active member of the Institute of Functional Medicine and Functional Pharmacy Medicine Alliance.

She has earned many certifications with NSU College of Pharmacy and the University of Florida's College of Pharmacy. She has been married for 25 years and loves every minute she gets to spend with her three college-age children and to play with her two golden retrievers. She also enjoys tennis, pickleball, and biking. She has always been athletic and was inducted into the Palm Beach County Sports Hall of Fame for her athletic accomplishments in high school.

Her goal is to help educate clients about the complex nature of the human body's digestive system and the simple language that the body uses to scream dysfunction. It's important to realize there is no simple antidote or magic pill to fix our harmful modern environment. The standard American diet, considered SAD, with its excess of sugar, refined carbohydrates, and trans fats are contributing to a rise in disease. Health doesn't happen overnight. It's imperative to understand that digestion is an issue that is central to our health!

Dr. Marilu Almeida Hunt, Pharm.D., CPh, CIHC, INHC
Gut Recharge, LLC
561-323-0365
Dr.Marilu@GutRecharge.com
www.gutrecharge.com
www.gutrecharge.com/Freewebinar/

Train Smarter, Not Harder! 3 Steps to Avoid Burnout and Optimize Performance!

Everyone wants to feel better. Having medical test results come back negative while still feeling lousy is a frustrating problem. This free webinar discusses how to take charge of your gut health, to live better, and win at life!

www.gutrecharge.com/Freewebinar/

Brittany Prince

Feel the Fear and Do It Anyways

"I understood myself only after I destroyed myself. And only in the process of fixing myself, did I know who I really was."

—Anonymous

We finally had a break from training. It was supposed to be a fun Saturday out on a boat with a group of classmates. It was a beautiful, sunny day. The weather was perfect. I remember getting on the boat, and then the next thing I knew, I was waking up someplace completely different to someone raping me. I started thinking to myself; this is not real. What's happening to me right now is just a dream. I was literally in and out of consciousness on a bed in a hotel room. I have no idea how I got there. In the distance, I could hear someone else talking, "Hey, what are you doing?" As I was lying there, my mind went blank. I was in shock. I didn't move, and I didn't yell. I just froze and let it happen. Why aren't I moving? I don't want this. I didn't ask for this. And just like that, it was over. He got what he wanted, while I died a little bit inside that day. I would never be the same again, and my journey had only just begun. He had not seen the last of me.

"Strength grows in the moments when you think you can't go on, but you keep going anyway."

I joined the Army in 2013. I was very excited to be a part of something bigger than myself. I knew it was going to change my life. However, I didn't think it was going to change so quickly and in such a drastic way.

I was sexually assaulted six months into my service during airborne school. I hid that secret for four months. Not a single person knew about it. I finally decided to report my assault and bring it to trial. It was a long and rough road. There were many low points for me during that process. I had friends, but no one truly understood what I was going through. It was a lonely process that made me pick up some unhealthy habits.

Drinking became my new outlet. It helped me cope with the feelings that were bottled up and the shame I felt from the assault. There were nights where my dreams felt so real. It was like my assault was happening all over again. However, that didn't stop me from my drinking because there were nights where the drinking helped me forget everything. I felt good again like a normal person.

The whole trial process tore me apart. It was like a waiting game, not knowing what was going to happen next. There were phone calls with lawyers and interviews that needed very specific details. It later put me into a downward spiral. I wasn't allowed to forget and move on. It was now my responsibility to remember every single tiny detail. For example: What was I looking at as I was lying in that hotel bed being assaulted? What time did the clock say? Was it daytime or nighttime? What did I hear on the TV in the background? How do I know he was having sex with me? Was I sure there was someone else in the room? The trial hadn't even started, and yet it felt as if it had. So, yes, the days were long, and my nights began with drinking. It was because, during those moments, there was nothing else that could help me. I felt defeated. I started going to therapy twice a week, but even that place was no longer a safe space for me.

I soon found out that the defense attorney had taken possession of my therapy records. I had been stripped of all my privacy. I began to feel like I was the bad guy in this. It all started to get very heavy for me emotionally. I didn't think I could handle this pressure anymore. I was at my breaking point. I just wanted it over.

I called my dad and told him I didn't want to go through with it anymore.

This is what he told me, "That's your decision to make. If you don't feel like you can move forward with it, then call it off. But just know if you call it off, you can't go back, and you may regret it the rest of your life. Brittany, I know you're hurting, but you need to feel the fear and do it anyway. This very well could happen to another woman if you don't hold him accountable." That conversation is what kept me grounded and reminded me why I was reporting it in the first place. I wasn't about to go down without a fight.

The trial finally came. It was like a pack of wolves tearing me apart, little by little. My character was put into question. There was a picture going around of me sitting on a guy's lap on a boat. He had his arm wrapped around my leg. I was being asked, "Why did you let him put his arm on you like that?" "Did you like it?" "Didn't you notice how his hand was placed on your leg?" I had no memories from that day. Therefore, this was the first time I saw the picture. The questions kept coming. I felt so attacked. I was the victim here, but they were eating me alive as if I was in the wrong. What did I get myself into? However, I dug deep inside myself and kept moving. I did the best I could with each question and just told my truth. That's all I could do. I was there for a purpose, and I wasn't about to give up.

There were new things that I also learned during the trial that I had no memory of. My assailant took me into the shower to not only clean me off but to also do other things to me. He then continued with me on the bed. He thought it was a "romantic" time. At least that's what he told everyone in court. The other thing I learned, the person who walked in on my assault (my only hard evidence) originally did not want to come forward and tell the truth of what happened. He wanted no part in court. Luckily, he had no choice because he was under oath.

I felt so much shame and anger learning those details. How could I be so betrayed by people who wore the same uniform as me? It was hard to stomach. On top of that, having lawyers trying to convince the jury that my assailant wasn't guilty made it even harder for me to respect the men in uniform.

When it was finally time for the verdict, God was on my side. **I WON!** He was found guilty and was dishonorably discharged from the military, on top of having to serve a couple of years. Now, I could really start healing.

You Have to Keep Moving Forward. Every Day Is a New Day with a Clean Slate.

I still struggled after the trial was over. Even though I won, my negative feelings from the assault were still there. I felt shame when putting on the uniform and also the hatred I had for men. I knew this wasn't going to be an overnight change. However, I didn't know how to move forward. I was stuck in the same mindset of being victimized. I did the best I could with what I had, and so I continued with therapy and eventually got brave enough to start group therapy. That's when things began to change for me. I realized that I was no longer alone and that there were many other women like me. I began to learn that by talking to others, it helped me get my feelings out in a healthy way. It made me want to take care of myself more so that one day I could help other women.

I started writing every day about anything that I was feeling. I would put it down on paper. It became my new outlet. Something where I could get my feelings out without sharing every detail with people. It made me feel more in command of myself, like I wasn't spiraling out of control anymore. Then two years after my assault, I finally wrote something and shared it with complete strangers during an event in town.

After I spoke, people came up to me afterward and thanked me for sharing. I had never felt so proud of myself. I will always cherish my first writing after my assault because it helped me realize that I am not defined by what happened to me.

Here's a little piece of my defining moment:

A Letter to My Dad

Dear Daddy,

It wasn't your fault.

You did nothing wrong. There was nothing you could have done.

Don't let those "what if's" play their song.

I know you lie awake at night wondering how you could've been better.

But that's one reason why I'm writing you this letter.

You taught me to be strong, to sing my song out loud in a crowd, and to be proud of who I am.

To stand tall and never let them see me fall.

You taught me that I have a choice in my life.

You're a father that I can look up to and learn what's right from wrong.

You've shown me a bond that can never be broken and a love that's ever so strong.

You've taught me that NO is a very powerful word that should never be taken lightly.

So, when he took that power away from me, I bowed my head disgracefully.

I remember you taught me that my body is my temple, and people need to respect it.

Why can't they learn it's okay to get rejected?

I never asked for it, this isn't on me, this hatred that I have is way beyond me.

But dad, you taught me that I'm better than that.

You told me that hate in the heart is no way to live, so it's time for me to let go and forgive.

I wasn't ready before, but I don't want to feel this pain anymore.

So, I FORGIVE HIM.

I'm okay now, dad. I'm safe and sound, though once was lost, I've now been found.

I just want to thank you from the bottom of my heart.

For being the amazing father that you are.

Without your guidance and your lessons of life,

My survivor inside would not have sufficed.

It's a process, and things won't change overnight. I had to get to rock bottom in order to find the strength inside myself. Only then was I able to start building myself back up and finding out who I really was.

These Are My Top Three Tactical Strategies to Combat Trauma.

1. You Can't Let Trauma Define Who You Are.

Yes, you are allowed to grieve the loss of the person you once were before your trauma happened, but don't let it consume you. Don't let it define who you are.

2. Learn from the Trauma and Keep Moving Forward.

Do not give up on yourself. It's going to be a rough road ahead. There may be times when you think you can't go on, but that's when you **HAVE** to keep moving. I promise there's a light at the end of the tunnel.

3. You ARE Capable of Handling Any Trauma.

Don't be so hard on yourself and give yourself grace. You are learning how to navigate the new person you are becoming. You are **STRONG**, you are **CAPABLE**, you **WILL** bounce back from this because you are **RESILIENT.**

In life, bad things will happen to you. When they do, you have three options. You can let it define you, you can let it destroy you, or you can let it strengthen you. We all have a fighter in us, so give that side a chance to fight for what you deserve.

Brittany Prince

Brittany Prince served in the United States Army from 2013-2018. During her time in the service, she was faced with a traumatic event that changed her life. In 2013, she was sexually assaulted by another service member. However, she still pushed forward and was able to put her offender on trial. By the Grace of God, she won. Since then, she has been a strong advocate in helping programs spread awareness of sexual assault/harassment in the military. She has worked alongside the Army's Sexual Harassment/ Assault Response and Prevention Program (SHARP). She has even spoken out about her assault during a few of their events. In 2017, she had her first baby, Lucas. It changed her life forever. It gave her new perspectives on life and what was really important. The following year, she was able to get out of the military. She became a stay-at-home mother, and in 2019, she had her second baby, Lyla. Brittany loved everything about being able to raise her own kids, but she still felt like there was something missing. She wanted to do more, so in 2020, she started her bachelor's degree from Liberty University, studying business (entrepreneurship). She eventually wants to have her own business helping women heal from their trauma. In 2021, she has now been given an opportunity to inspire others by telling her story in a book called *Overcoming Mediocrity — Empowered Women*. She not only wants to inspire others to be their best selves, but she wants to teach her kids that there is no obstacle they can't get through.

Brittany Prince
Trauma2Triumph21@gmail.com

4 Steps to Triumph Over Trauma

If at any time during your military career you've been sexually assaulted, this guide will provide you with four simple strategies and helpful resources to confidently take your assault to trial. I've also included my email address for anyone who wants to talk or needs some support.

https://bit.ly/2R7tIY6

Tess Booker

Life Is Working for You

I am a woman of many passions, full of life, and curiosity. As a child, I thought I could save the world with a childlike love and wonder of how all things could be made beautiful. I literally saw the world as "eating rainbows and pooping butterflies." I saw abundance and love, but my life did not align with it. My life felt like fear, rejection, abandonment, and shame. My response to others became my reality, which I believed to be true. The world I saw was not the earth I was living in. If I could put this in context, after watching the *Wonder Woman* sequels, while it is Hollywood and are just movies, it occurred to me that I related to this story. I am Wonder Woman. Can I really say that out loud and have people turn their heads? I know you are too. You may just not realize it yet. Do you have an inner confidence that you know in your heart that you are created from God and for purpose? Wonder Woman had that inner confidence, in which her mother knew deeply but did not want others to *know who she was*. Wonder Woman did not succumb to the fear her mother had. You must watch the movie. I would also love to stop all of the suffering in the world. I am considered a hypersensitive person or an empath. It is exhausting being with people who are hurting. I find myself taking on others' hurts and identities as my own. While the labels validate and justify me to carry the negative energy. In contrast, it became my excuse not to take ownership of my own energy. I found myself disconnected from who I am, chasing the results I thought would make me somehow more credible to help others, chasing knowledge, and obsessed with personal growth. I realized there is a huge gap between what I want and what I do and have. Because I feel deeply and I am empathetic, I was on an emotional rollercoaster. When does all the knowledge, affirmations, prayers, and personal growth really get results not driven by how I feel? I found myself in constant frustration, overwhelmed with not enough time, not enough money, and little attention to my own needs. I have had amazing wins in my life, yet I have patterns of disqualifying my inner being and the fact that I was never enough, feeling responsible for the whole world and all the brokenness in the world, and not owning my life. I was giving away my power rather than embracing my gifts.

There are moments when you look back and realize that life is working for you. This is my story behind my passion and my power to profit. Steve Jobs says, *"You can't connect the dots looking forward; you can only connect them looking backward. So, you must trust that the dots will somehow connect in your future. You have to trust in something — your gut, destiny, and life."* I realized that my being was not aligning with what I could do or be. The journey began in the summer of 1990 but was not really understood until 2015. I had an opportunity to serve and be in the communities/orphanages with Mother Teresa. I was young and had no idea of that impact on my life. Upon returning to the United States, months later, I found myself magnifying our culture of consumers, not satisfied, complaining of trivial problems. I was overwhelmed at the number of choices I had, just in the grocery store. While in India, I experienced those who have few choices, financially stuck in a caste system, and tortured because of their beliefs. I was overwhelmed with the extreme poverty and lack of water, nutrition, and hundreds of cases of elephantiasis and leprosy rampant in the streets. However, my experience with the families and those I lived with was that they were grateful, hospitable, and displayed a loving culture. I never felt more love, which was in contrast to the lack and the hate within the holy wars and the resistance to unity. I became confused about who I was and what I believed. Years later, I went to Haiti with my teenage daughter to give her an experience outside of herself. At the time, I was in business for myself, dabbling in network marketing, with high expectations to soar but miserable in the process. This trip was life-altering for me. It was another dramatic shift in my perceptions and resistance to resources and money. It occurred to me that the experience I had in Haiti was not different from India. There were the same problems with poverty, hate about religions and ideas, suppressed people, and a lack of resources. The difference was my response and the meaning that I gave to those experiences. Upon returning home from India, it took me a long time to be okay with the desire to want more for my life. What I found is that my wants left me miserable because I did not have what I wanted. My deep desire to show influence, love, compassion, and unity but despised the resources to do so. This was a pivotal moment to change what I was doing to be resourceful and leave a legacy with people. The belief "I cannot have money and be spiritual" was the lie I had to face. I realized I had an opportunity to help the orphans or those in the slums of India. I could have decided to adopt a child in India. However, I was so focused on all the things I could not respond to, that I limited my own impact, even if it felt small. That mindset cost years of my life, ignoring opportunities where I could have served with what I had. Upon coming back from Haiti, my new decision was made, "I am going home to make a Sh*%$ load of money." WHY? So, I could help a lot of people.

That led me into more frustration. I still did not get it. I dove into the process with resistance. I began asking and telling myself, "Does this really mean I must get visible and be rejected over and over? This is taking so long. Network marketing doesn't work, and my teams don't understand me." I was hustling. I still lacked. I got some wins along the way but could not celebrate my wins. What I was inspired to have and what I needed to do, was now the most stressful thing in my life. I was again faced with the chasing process. I felt like an eagle one day and a worm the next. I was waiting to be eaten by the eagle. I call it the entrepreneurial carrousel. I was led by my feelings up and down. I sought training from every influencer I could find. I also invested a lot of money and time with coaches; Brendan Burchard, Tony Robbins, David Bayer, John Maxwell, Rob Sperry, Eric Worre, and many others. I followed many spiritual leaders and attained knowledge. I was exhausted and did not feel respected by my peers. I caught myself in a whirlwind of having to prove myself. Where was my passion? Will resources and money even be satisfying? Chasing money does not make sense. However, my dreams and who I want to serve cost me resources. This ultimately is *mediocracy*, not moving in either direction. I was stuck between fear of success and fear of failure. How is it I can have these amazing experiences? I lived in another country, survived cancer, been through dozens of triathlons, survived a marriage that fell apart, healed and powerfully married years later, raised beautiful kids, and built multiple businesses. I have faced my fears and triumphed many times. I now was looking at my fear of success. I had underlying beliefs that repeatedly kept popping up in my life. This revealed to me that it was not a lack of discipline or heart. This is me sabotaging my success and profitability through stinking thinking.

Experience and process ultimately are two ways we tend to respond to our life and circumstances, the power we give, and how we perceive beliefs. This experience in high school was a deep-seated belief, rooted deeply in how I showed up in life and business. I was the captain of the swim team, and we won the state championship. However, I was publicly disqualified because of protocols. I did not celebrate that win. I felt that I disappointed my team because of a protocol in place that I failed. There were many experiences in my life where I felt the systems did not work for me, no matter what I did. I always felt guilty for my success and feared leaving others behind. My two beliefs were: "Systems don't work" and "If I win or celebrate my win, I will leave others behind." There was no wonder my process was not working. I had to make a new powerful decision. I create the space for others to also experience freedom. Although everything has processes and protocols, I do not have to do them perfectly to win. I boldly do the work and go through the process. I allow it to work for me and shift as necessary. I learn, grow, and embrace my success. It is important to feel relaxed in order to receive love, abundance, wealth, and prosperity. This knowledge is making things work out for me and those around me.

I found that there are some keys to discovering purpose that has given me clarity about my experiences and the process required to live a life of fulfillment, whatever stage of life you are in. It is important to understand that your life is purposeful. The destination is not the point, but being positioned, living each day and each moment knowing that life is working for you, so you are able to give and receive. It is constant, like ocean waves going in and out of our breath. Breathing in is no less important than breathing out. Your truths, experience, and process determine the life you desire to have. I have spent twenty years implementing and teaching these principles, and now with an established business as an alignment coach, I continue to help position direct paths of clarity within life and business.

Many women are inspired by these principles being addressed, but the reality is most entrepreneurs can either be inspired, have a vision, and struggle with implementing to get the results they desire, or work hard and find no purpose and are not satisfied in their hustle and creating. What I found is that you cannot separate your spiritual being from your business. It is essential to a profitable life around your business.

Knowing your **Position**, including where you stand, your stories, desires, beliefs, convictions, and feelings are your guide in making powerful decisions. It is the essence from which all else flows. It is the life within you that expresses itself in your life and business. Be comfortable in your journey to discover and find your unique passion.

It will reveal the **Power** with which you can now trust and align with, whom I call God. Dare to uncover your limiting beliefs through the source of infinite energy and beautiful love that is within you. Learn to be decisive, clear, and trust yourself and what is the divine in you.

This is your place of **Profitability**. Be willing to take imperfect action, gain credibility and begin to influence at a greater level. Decide to not overthink or be overwhelmed in your daily life because you now can confidently lead with authenticity and purpose. Having a clear vision and message to reach those looking for you establishes your branding. Your profitability will come with less stress and more grace.

Once you discover your purpose and position yourself through your stories, you will find your passion, demonstrate your divine power, release fears and limiting beliefs, and embrace your profitability. Being an empowered woman is not about being stronger, more perfect, or saving the world. It is about you know who you are, how you show up, and who you are serving. It is in your spiritual alignment that your business becomes resourceful. Upon this journey, you will reveal and achieve ultimate fulfillment and influence in this deep love of life and legacy.

Tess Booker

Tess is happily married to her best friend. She has three amazing children and considers herself blessed to have them all call her mom. Her passion illuminates the love of life. She enjoys the divine connections. She continues to seek places of gratitude and wonder that inspire her to help serve others and experience life living practically here and now, as well as having a vision for her future. Tess is the founder of Inspired Living. She's a driven entrepreneur who values her own personal growth. She knows the pain, frustrations, and fears that entangle and hold us back from which we desire. She is relentless and committed to her freedom. She has many years of hands-on years of experience in the network marketing industry and continues to serve others, as she inspires women to find their stories, their power, and profit in their life and business. She is the kind of person you want in your corner.

Tess spends her time dedicated to her own alignments and being empowered in her life, and enhancing the lives of others. She has compiled and authored an amazon published book titled *"Tess Booker and Friends, Inspired Lives"* this process and coaching of others to write their stories and seek out their journey empowered, purpose revealed through their tragedies and into their own empowerment.

She loves to compete in triathlons, connecting to others, and being with her family. She is an established entrepreneur, published Amazon author, triathlete, speaker, and transformational coach. Her coaching draws out your unique story to help you align your spiritual vision, helping you to embrace the power within you to implement and profit within your life and business.

"When we speak from our experiences, you are not just giving information, you are releasing power of transformation."

—Bill Johnson

Tess Booker
Inspired Living LLC
357 49th Loop
Springfield, OR 97478
541-337-4078
TessBookerInspiredLiving@gmail.com
www.TessBooker.com

Think Outside of Your Box

Direct Path to Clarity, you can have an aligned successful business. It is not as hard as you think to re-wire your brain.

www.TessBooker.com

Terri Lynn Yanke

Think Bigger! Find Your Purpose, Live with Passion, and Experience Everything

My childhood was not bad. It was just lonely. I was an only child for the first six years of my life, with my siblings being 6 and 13 years younger than myself. I lived in rural Wisconsin but not on a farm. There was one house next to my house with a couple of children who were also younger than me. Beyond that, the only thing you could see in all directions were cornfields. To go anywhere, we had to drive a long distance. My mom drove me to preschool, dance classes, and swim classes. I knew from these experiences that it was fun to be around kids my own age. I could not wait to get on a bus that would take me to school, a place where I would have friends to play with.

School became my happy place. I no longer minded those alone times at home. I knew I would be returning the next day and be back with my friends at school. As kindergarten turned into first grade, my friendships deepened, and I enjoyed a comfortable sense of belonging. Then my world abruptly changed. My school friends were yanked away from me. I still remember the day when the local newspaper arrived in late summer with this heartbreaking news. The newspaper was where I would find out who would be my teacher and which of my friends would be in my class. I could not find my name listed at my school. Was this just a mistake? This same newspaper also listed the bus route. I discovered that my bus would now be going to a different school. Sure enough, there was my name listed under this school! I did not know the teacher. I did not know one other child in my class. I cried very hard, knowing that I would not be seeing my friends again. I was so sad. I was also very afraid. I would be going to a school that I had never been to before and be with people I did not know. Fearful thoughts kept going through my head. *Would they accept me? Would they like me? Would I make new friends?*

The first day of school for second grade arrived. I boarded the bus that morning with different scenarios going through my head of how the day would go. None of them were good. I was physically shaking, feeling so scared of what the day would bring. I got off the bus to see kids greeting one another, laughing, and gathering in groups around the playground before school started. It made me miss my friends at my old school even more and made me feel very alone. I had no one to talk to. No one talked to me. I did not even know where to go. My eyes started to tear up as I wandered into the school to find my classroom. My new teacher was there and must have seen the tears in my eyes. She welcomed me with a big smile and showed me to my desk. She went out of her way to make me feel better and to let me know that this was where I belonged. She helped make my fears go away. I will always remember how good this teacher made me feel. From this point on in my life, I started going out of my way to make people feel welcome and that they belonged. I became known for my smile.

I also learned that I could make new friends. With a little time and effort, I became part of the group of kids that gathered on the playground. School again became my favorite place to be. I enjoyed deepening my friendships and the comfortable sense of belonging that came with another passing year. And then it happened again! For fourth and fifth grade, I ended up going to yet another different school. And believe it or not, it happened again! In sixth grade, I went to another school. Each time I learned, I would be going to a different school, which made me feel hurt and sad that I would not be able to see my friends. However, I was no longer afraid. I had developed confidence in myself. I knew that eventually, at my new school, everything would turn out to be OK and that I would make new friends again.

This childhood experience of losing my friends and sense of belonging every two years and the confidence that I developed from it kept me brave and strong throughout my life. My effort to make people feel welcome and that they belong helped me to make new friends. I was able to move to faraway places for different and better jobs. I was able to travel by myself and experience new cultures. It allowed me to climb the corporate ladder and be a success in my career. It gave me the strength to leave a job that was stifling. It gave me the courage to leave bad situations and bad relationships. I knew I did not need to settle and that I could pick up and start over to make things better. I ended up doing this several times in my life. I was not afraid to think bigger. It empowered me to be able to live life with passion and experience it more fully.

Never did I need this strength more than when after twenty years of marriage, my husband surprised me by asking for a divorce. I had left my job in corporate America a few years before and was doing some consulting at this time. I felt that the only way I would be able to be secure would be to go back to my corporate career. I updated my resume and accepted a job offer that would take me from Connecticut to Dallas, Texas. I could not help but feel some of those same anxious feelings that I had as a kid getting on a bus to go to a new school. Now, I had some even scarier thoughts since I was an adult in a very new situation. I would be alone for the first time in twenty years. Different than the previous times, I did not have parents, a husband, or a child to come home to. I was also moving to a place I really did not know much about, nor did I know anyone that lived there. I told myself that I have done this before, and I can do this again. I was not afraid to think bigger. I had confidence that I would figure things out.

It was not as easy to make friends being older and single in a new city like it was when I was younger. I discovered Meetup and started a singles group to selfishly find friends. I made sure members of this group felt welcome and that they belonged. Having this group allowed me to live again with passion and experience everything. I created events for whatever I wanted to do and wherever I wanted to go. I was able to make some great friends, and I was not alone in discovering my new city. Just like school was my happy place as a child, the events that I organized for my group became my new happy place. In less than three years, my group grew to almost 3000 people, and my events kept getting bigger and bigger.

While things were going well for me at my job, the company I worked for was bought out, and a new owner came in and trimmed the workforce. Many people, including myself, were let go. I thought to myself, here I go again. I will need to find a new job, most likely move again, and start over in a new city. I did not even think I had a different choice. I updated my resume and searched for my next job. I was soon flying to different cities for interviews. It was so hard for me to feel any excitement in exploring these job possibilities. I no longer had the passion for doing what I have been doing most of my life. I knew I needed to make a change. I had always wanted to have a business of my own, but I did not know what that looked like. In talking about this with my friends, they looked at me strangely and said, "Terri, you do events?"

I finally found my purpose. Yes, I do events! It was right before my eyes, and I did not see it. It took my friends to tell me what I should do, but it fit perfectly. In thinking back, I have been doing events my whole life, both personally and professionally, through my job. I felt so happy to have clarity that I was going to do something that I knew I was passionate about and exceptionally good at doing. I enjoy nothing better than being able to pull a group of people together and make sure they have a great experience. I soon discovered in starting my event business that I could give extra value to my business event clients based on my education and work experience, something that not many event planners could do. I decided to focus on business events, where I could help my clients get the results they want while creating the right environment and memorable attendee experiences that will make them want to do business with them.

I now feel what I have gone through, overcome, and learned from my experiences can be helpful to others in scary situations. I also wish for others to feel how good I feel since stumbling upon my purpose and passion and would like to help them find theirs. I know I can create magic for my clients, and I even find myself using what has empowered me to be able to help my clients get the results they want. **Do not be afraid to think bigger.** Everyone is afraid at one time or another. Do not let this stop you from reaching for something that will be better for you. Push through this feeling and take action to move yourself forward, and you will find that the fear will go away. I know that having events can be scary and even overwhelming. I help my clients by taking the strategy and planning parts of the event off their shoulders. I can share and follow best practices to help them feel assured they will get the results they want. I can bring them ideas to elevate their event to be something better and bigger than they ever thought.

Find your purpose. When you know what your purpose is and can live doing it, you will be happier. Your life will have more meaning, and work is enjoyable. It is also good to know what your purpose and goals are for other areas of your life so that you can work to achieve them. I help my clients identify what their purpose is to have an event. Knowing what the purpose is, makes it easier to strategically build the event to achieve this. It will also help my clients to get the results they want.

Live with passion and experience everything. Find and do the things that make you happy, proud, enthusiastic, and fulfilled. Use all your senses to experience everything around you. You will shine to others, and it will make you feel good. You will have great memories to think back on. My passion for doing events shows to my client. They cannot help feeling it too when we work together. My company tagline is "Create Experiences Not Just Events." To create the best experience possible, I draw upon all five senses. I help create the right environment with a memorable attendee experience that will both make the client look good, and the attendee want to do business with them.

No extraordinary result ever came from a mediocre effort. My path to my purpose took me a while. There were several scary things that I had to face and move forward from, but I learned not to be afraid to think bigger. Now that I have my own business that I can do from anywhere, I decided to make one additional change in my life. I packed up that same car that took me from Connecticut to Dallas and drove it to Madison, WI, to be closer to family. Do not be afraid to find your own purpose, live with passion, and experience everything. THINK BIGGER!

Terri Lynn Yanke

Terri Lynn Yanke has been doing events her whole life without even realizing it. She did not make it official until 2018 when she launched her company Eventful Advantage LLC with the tag line "Create Experiences Not Just Events." Now known as the Biz Event Wizard + Experience Visionary, her focus is to help her clients get the results they want with the right attendee experiences that will create income, whether the event is in-person, virtual, or hybrid. Prior to having her own company, Terri Lynn earned a BBA in Marketing and Management and an MBA in Marketing. She climbed the corporate ladder in retail/wholesale, with over 20 years as an apparel executive for several well-known companies. From managing buyers to selecting the right merchandise for stores to managing designers and merchandisers to creating product lines and bringing them to market, she used events to build her business. Her career gave her the opportunity to live in many different places and travel the world.

She utilizes these experiences and her strong business foundation to make her events stand out and to help her clients achieve better results than they ever thought possible. Pulling people together is something Terri Lynn loves to do, and she has a history of being successful at it. In addition to her events business, she is the Managing Director of eWomenNetwork-Madison, where she started a chapter after finding out that Madison did not have one. She produces and facilitates two events per month while building this community. Terri Lynn wants to educate business owners about the power of events to grow their income in the quickest way possible and the experiences that need to be created to do so. She enjoys speaking to different groups and sharing best practices to have the most successful events possible.

Terri Lynn Yanke
Eventful Advantage LLC
5471 Liverpool Street
Waunakee, WI 53597
203-260-8336
Terri.Yanke@EventfulAdvantage.com
https://EventfulAdvantage.com

5 Event Best Practices to Get the Results You Want!

Business Events are one of the quickest ways to keep your current clients engaged, gain additional clients, increase your sales, and expand your brand awareness, all at one time. Do not be afraid to think bigger! It is not unusual to 10X the money you usually make from just one event. These results do not just happen. You need to strategically build the event to make it a success. Follow these Five Event Best Practices to Get the Results You Want.

https://mailchi.mp/83374695840e/5-event-best-practices

Sharon LaPointe

An Open Dialogue

"All truths are easy to understand once they are discovered: the point is to discover them."

—Galileo Galilei

Girl, do I have a story to tell you!

Did you know that you can go back as far as when you were five years old and remember events in your life? Sometimes your memories will be clear, and sometimes they will be cloudy. I remember things that happened to me at age five that were horrible to experience, and at that time, I didn't know those events would alter the trajectory of my life. How could you know at age five the impact certain events would have on your future?

From age five to nine, I was sexually molested. One day I got the courage to tell my parents. There I was, sitting at the kitchen table. My arms were wrapped around my body, frightened of what would happen next. As I spilled the beans to my parents, they looked at me without expression. When I was done, they told me to go outside and play. That was it! Nothing else was said.

Fast forward to age 14. Being an adolescent comes with raging hormones, rebelliousness, mood swings, sarcasm, selfishness, and recklessness. The list goes on and on. Not knowing anything about the world and human existence beyond that of a 14-year-old, I didn't know what I didn't know. As a result, I behaved accordingly. I engaged in drugs and partying. I hitchhiked all over the country, on my own, and with friends. I sneaked out of the house late at night and did not come home, sometimes until 6 a.m. in the morning.

Eventually, I ended up in the foster care system in Massachusetts. I became a ward of the state and got myself kicked out of all three foster homes. The conditions of my departure were not pleasant. At the last one, my social worker told me there was no other place for me to go but the Amherst Shelter for Wayward Kids in Amherst, Massachusetts. So, off I went. It wasn't until my senior year in high school that a good friend took pity on me and asked his parents if I could come live with them. This would become my 4th and final foster placement. A few months later, I drove my car into a tree and almost killed myself. My social worker was called in again, and she announced to everyone, "Sharon is almost 18: There is nothing more we can do for her now. We are no longer responsible for you. You have to figure your own life out now." So, I went back to my parents. However, my reckless hitchhiking, drug use, and partying continued throughout the rest of my adolescence.

Fast forward to age 30. I had a son who was 11 and a daughter, age six. They were the absolute joy and love of my life. My husband and I bought our first house after years of financial struggle by working two and three jobs and taking all the steps needed to buy a home. Life was moving along great, except for the occasional upsets and dysfunctional events that most families experience when raising kids and having dual careers.

Nine years later, I was sitting at my kitchen table. My 15-year-old daughter had been hibernating in her room for weeks. As she walked into the kitchen to get something to eat, I looked at her and noticed that she was growing tall. What a big girl! I also noticed that she was blossoming in other ways. I thought to myself, "When did that happen?" A few days later, she said to me: "I'm sick, and I keep throwing up." I took her to the family doctor. There we were, sitting in a private room, joking, having fun, sharing our dog's funny moments while waiting for our doctor to come back with the test results. The doctor walked in and said to her: "Congratulations, you're pregnant!"

I never saw that coming! I looked at the doctor and said, "She can't have a kid. She's only 15." He said, "Girls in third world countries have kids all the time around the age of 14." We left to go home. On the way, I said to her, "Please consider having an abortion. You're too young to have a kid, and it will alter your life dramatically."

She did not get an abortion. However, I cried for about a month before I told myself that we would make this work. Not more than a week after I came to terms with this situation, my son came to us and said, "Um, my girlfriend is pregnant." At first, I was OK with this because he was 20 and an adult. However, he was still living at home, with no job and no college in his future. Two weeks later, my son's girlfriend was with our family doctor to determine her due date. He said that her due date was around October 10th and then said: "How funny is that. Your daughter is due around the end of September. Wouldn't it be great if they both gave birth at the same time?" As I looked at him, I thought to myself, "I have to find another doctor!" Both grandkids were born two weeks apart, became best friends, and interacted with each other as if they were siblings.

By 2006, we had sold our first home, built our dream home, and shared the house with our two kids and two grandkids. A year later, in October 2007, I was diagnosed with a rare and fast-growing tumor, called Endometrial Stromal Sarcoma, or uterine cancer. Can you imagine hearing those words? I felt that I was being handed a death sentence. I underwent two major surgeries, a radical hysterectomy, and radiation treatments five days a week for seven weeks. This made it very difficult for me to eat or work. I lost a lot of weight, and I looked like I was dying.

I was unwilling to accept a death sentence and decided to fight for my life. What really had me adamant about remaining on this planet was the thought of my husband moving on with his life with another woman and thinking he would be happy without me. There is no way that I could allow that to happen! I got into action and explored alternative medicines and healing techniques. I became vegan for a year, exercised, and took care of my well-being, both physically and mentally. I cut back on work and totally focused on myself. Without my health, I knew that I had nothing, and nothing else would matter.

While I was dealing with all of this, our economy went into recession. I had gotten my real estate license in 2004 and had been killing it until I got sick. However, my husband got laid off, and things began to fall apart. We had to sell our dream home, losing thousands of dollars. Our dream home had 3000 square feet. In February 2009, we moved into a rented 1-bedroom condo with only 765 square feet. Despite the loss and our radically changed circumstances, I never gave up. The following month, all the real estate deals I had pending finally closed. I earned $25,000.00 in commissions that month.

My family and I spent the next four years as renters, working every day, almost seven days a week, to get back into homeownership. My husband and I were in a tumultuous relationship and separated multiple times. At the end of 2012, again separated, I was angry and wondering about the meaning of my life. What was I really here for? I had $500 in my bank account, and my real estate business generated only $40k that year. That wasn't enough to buy a home or support my family on my own. I was at the point where I decided that my life needed to change and mean something more than what it had become. I took a leap of faith and signed up for the Landmark Forum.

That Friday evening, sitting in my chair with 150 other people in The Forum, we were given a homework assignment. It was to write a letter to anyone in our life with whom we felt our relationship was not complete. We were invited to clean up the messes we had created in our lives. On my way home, I was resisting doing that assignment. I was thinking, "I haven't done anything wrong. They are the ones who did me wrong!" Two hours later, I was lying in bed and decided to write a letter to my husband. I emptied out all of my thoughts about him onto two pages. After I had nothing left to write, I went back and read the letter to myself several times. What I discovered about myself is profound. I was insecure, resentful, angry, mad, sad, and behaved like a martyr. What's worse, I had been blaming my husband, kids, friends, and colleagues for all the negative thoughts and feelings I had about them. It was all their fault, not mine!

As I kept looking at myself, I was mortified. Saturday morning, I drove back to the Forum for Day 2, and on my way, I called my husband and said: "All these years, I blamed you for everything that was bad and wrong in my life. I made myself a victim, and I made you responsible for my insecurities and my happiness. I want you to know that you were never responsible for that, and I regret I did that." At that moment, as I said all that, I began to cry. He said to me, "I always knew that, and I never mustered the courage to ask you to think differently." And then we were both crying.

Putting myself into coaching and getting present with my own behavior has been life-changing for me. I've had many successes and accomplishments in my life, but until now, they have always been driven by my need to prove that others were wrong about me. My attitude has been: "I'll show you." I made all the trauma in my life mean that I was not good enough, smart enough, or pretty enough that I am not the one, and I don't matter! I compared myself unfavorably to others. I made myself bad and wrong my entire life.

Now, I know what I didn't know. Utopia doesn't exist outside of me. It exists within me, and I am free to experience it moment by moment. That five-year-old little girl created a story about herself, and she would always find the evidence for it. I am no longer that girl! I am now free to create a new story for my life. My life's circumstances and experiences no longer define me as a human being. I am in charge of my own growth and expansion. I now live my life by my own design, moment by moment.

There are a multitude of books, courses, coaches, training, and development resources out there for you, and you get to choose the one that works best for you. For me, the philosophy and practices I learned in the Landmark Forum have served me the best. It really takes something to pull your own life forward once you decide that mediocrity is not an option.

Sharon LaPointe

When Sharon LaPointe was a child, she created a story about who she was to others and believed this to be her truth. With a relentless spirit to prove others wrong, she quickly learned that to have the life she wanted. She would have to create it.

To put that into perspective, she developed a strong work ethic when she began working at the age of 14. She put herself through college, earning a bachelor's degree in legal studies. Her adolescent experiences and interaction with law enforcement and the court system drove her passion for becoming an advocate for those who had no voice of their own.

She began to achieve her goals through entrepreneurial outlets. After graduating from college, she worked as a paralegal for several years. She then became a Certified Supreme Court Volunteer Mediator, a crucial step that led her to become a professional guardian serving the elderly community and ultimately a VA Federal Fiduciary, serving 100% disabled veterans. This path forged the opportunity for her to own her own paralegal business serving pro-se litigants.

Sharon expanded her talents into becoming a pool hall/bar owner and a realtor while owning her paralegal business. Within one year of receiving her real estate license, she became a broker. She now owns and operates a small boutique real estate office and a home stage and redesigns business, in which she thrives in.

Sharon's commitment to public service has morphed into the creation of a non-profit project called "From Drab to Fab." Her team project provides an opportunity to have a free consultation with two rooms staged for qualified families or individuals looking to transform their living space.

Sharon enjoys coaching others on how to practice the art of self-generating a creative life by building confidence, courage, and full self-expression through creativity.

Sharon LaPointe

First Impressions Home Stage & Redesign

600 Cleveland Street, #232

Clearwater, FL 33755

407-906-5967

Info@1stImpressionDesign.com

www.1stImpressionDesign.com

You Never Get a Second Chance to Make a First Impression

Building courage, confidence, and full self-expression through creativity!

www.1stImpressionDesign.com

Tonya Stokes Ford

Escaped the Black Hole:
And Lived to Tell the Tale

There I was, smack dab in the middle of my worst nightmare. I was now freebasing cocaine on a daily basis. How did my life get so completely derailed? I was in a downward spiral into a black hole.

Family

I grew up an only child in a two-parent home. My fondest childhood memory was of my mom kneeling with me, teaching me to pray before bedtime. Never in my wildest dreams did I know that *prayer* would be my lifeline.

My family had attended church every Sunday. We were very active in church life. My mom played the piano for two choirs. One was an adult choir that my father directed, and the other was a children's choir with 90 children. I was 12 and sang in the choir. I once earned a lapel pin for a year of perfect Sunday School attendance. We were involved in many other church activities.

After graduating from high school, I attended Bowie State College… *Then,* the College was not accredited, and it had no football team. Bowie was nowhere near the bustling city it is now. I was done with the little backwoods College and ready to start working earning my own money.

By the time I was twenty, I had a "good Government job," my own car (with no car note), and my own apartment — life was very good.

The Next 10 Years

I freebased cocaine (coke) for ten years of my life. I call them the lost years. Freebasing is a fancy word for smoking a pure formula of cocaine.

When a childhood friend became my next-door neighbor, he introduced me to freebasing. He eventually also introduced me to his dealer. The three of us became very close friends. They were my smoking partners. Soon after, they taught me how to cut cocaine with baking soda and "cook it up," preparing a "rock" for smoking. A "rock" is what it's called after cooking because it's smooth, round, and very hard.

My dealer called one evening to say he was coming over. When he got there, he announced, "I'm here to teach you how to smoke properly."

In the 1970s, cocaine was the drug of choice for the elite, affluent, celebrities, and high rollers. This meant it was an expensive habit to have. Learning to smoke it properly made it worth the money spent.

My dealer was the cocaine master, and I was his excellent apprentice. I graduated Magna Cum Laude from The Art of Freebasing 101.

The crazy stupid thing about smoking coke is the best hit is that first hit and the high only lasts 10 to 15 seconds. Did that stop me from smoking cocaine? No.

Remember Len Bias? While playing basketball for the University of Maryland, he was named a first-team All-American. He was also the *second* NBA draft pick for the Boston Celtics in 1986.

I heard of another dealer whose product was good. As I was leaving his apartment, I saw a familiar face coming toward me. It was Len Bias. "Hey Len," I said. "Hey," he responded. We didn't speak because we knew each other. I knew he played basketball for the University of Maryland. And he was responding to a fan. He entered the apartment I had just left.

"They" were right. This coke was *better* than good. Later, as I dressed for work, I heard an announcer on the TV say:

"Sad news this morning, basketball player Len Bias is dead at 22 from cardiac arrhythmia, induced by a cocaine overdose."

It shocked me! We bought coke from the same place the night before. This young man was dead, and I was alive. Did **that** stop me from smoking cocaine? No.

The boldest thing I've ever done was to smuggle my pipe and a rock onto an airplane. I was traveling with co-workers to one of our Regional Offices in Cleveland, Ohio. I'd never been to Cleveland. The workday ended at 4:30 p.m. All-day, I anticipated going to my hotel room and getting high. 4:30 couldn't come fast enough.

At the end of the workday, someone suggested we go rest for an hour, then meet in the lobby and go "Have a nice dinner on Uncle Sam's tab." I quickly made up an excuse — I had the worst headache. I was going to my room, shower, and take a nap. I'd eat later.

Smoking cocaine makes you super paranoid. My mind kept telling me there were hidden cameras in the room or that others could smell my smoking coke under the door. I didn't feel safe, like at home. The paranoia made me smoke much faster than normal, and when that was gone, I wanted more.

The Friendliest People

Our hotel was in a nice area of the city. You could clearly see that in the taxi ride from the airport.

I made a right turn out of the hotel and started walking until I reached a distressed-looking part of the city. Then I started looking for a guy who had *that look* like he'd know where to score (buy) some coke.

Finally, I approached someone and asked if he knew where I could get a "working fifty." (A "rock" of coke big enough to cut into smaller pieces, so you could smoke some and sell some to make some of your money back.) He acknowledged he did, and we started walking.

I followed this guy through back streets and alleyways until we finally came to an apartment. He knocked on the door in code, three knocks, one knock, two knocks. The door opened into a brightly lit room, with people sitting on beanbag chairs around the room getting high.

There was a man in the kitchen, sitting on a stool next to the stove. I was introduced as Tonya, the lady from D.C., "What can I *do you for* Baby Girl?" I told him what I wanted. He handed me the product.

I handed him the money. I said, "thank you," and started toward the door. "Where you going Baby Girl? Sit for a minute, take a couple of hits, make sure you like it before you leave."

"But I didn't bring my pipe with me," I said. "Not a problem, come over here and sit next to me for a minute." To my amazement, he showed me how to make a pipe out of a soda can.

I stayed for two hours, smoking from my makeshift pipe. I could not have asked to meet a more friendly group of people than I met that night.

On that trip to Cleveland, I could have been robbed, raped, and/or killed. The people who I traveled with would have only known that I simply vanished. The last time they would have seen me was Wednesday at 4:30 p.m. My mom would have been devastated. We were very close. Did that thought make me quit smoking cocaine? No. All I wanted was the next high.

In my heart of hearts, I *wanted* to stop smoking, but the pull of the Black Hole was too great. I abandoned all those years of being in the church — *Gone*. The Bible says God never leaves us or forsakes us. I was the one that left Him. Even in my foolishness, God kept me safe. God in His infinite **Mercy** allowed me enough lucid moments for me to see that something **had** to change or I was going to die. I did what my mama taught me so long ago, I prayed. "Jesus, I **want** to quit smoking, but I love it. I *love* **everything** about it. If I am going to quit, it's all up to You. I trust and believe You *can*, and You *will* help me. Amen."

Performing Fellatio on the Devil

I had a visitor one day, a girlfriend I hadn't seen in a long time. We had smoked together before, and I trusted her. We were reminiscing about the good old days. Then, out of the blue, she says, "Tea (some friends call me Tea), you know what they call freebasing now?" "No, what is it called?"

She said we were performing fellatio on the devil. Then in my ear, as if Satan himself were saying, "…and you're so **good** at it." ***That did it!*** God knew that would be *it* for me. I gave the rest of the coke to her, took my glass pipe to the sink, wrapped it in a tea towel, took a hammer, and smashed it to smithereens. God knew that image and those words would be enough for me to quit cold turkey. He answered my prayer and took away the desire and craving for cocaine altogether. I like saying I went through the 5-step **J.E.S.U.S.** Drug Program.

Jesus is the

Everlasting way to

Stop

Using

Substance drugs

Escaping the Black Hole meant that I was free. I was no longer engulfed in the darkness of the Black Hole and no longer tethered to the cocaine. I was able to share with my dealer how God delivered me, also that I was praying for him.

I became involved in the church again. For the next ten years, I designed the church bulletins each week. I was the director of a children's choir for a while.

I now serve as a Sabbath School Superintendent at my present church.

But, my greatest joy was being close with my mom again. She was 80 years wise, and I didn't want her living alone. So, we agreed to move in together.

We were avid Scrabble players. I called her one day and said, "Put on your Scrabble hat. I'll be home in ten minutes." She met me at the door with a hat on that had the word SCRABBLE stapled to it.

Some days, we'd have Scrabble Marathons that went into the wee hours of the morning. She'd say, "Just one more game pleeeze — we're both retired and don't have to get up early?!"

Her birthday was Halloween, and for her 90th birthday, I took her to Chuck E. Cheese. She had a grand time watching all the kiddies in their costumes, hopped up on sugar, running all over the place. I'm so glad we spent that birthday doing something she loved; because nine months later, she was gone.

In her late 80s, I had started praying that God would allow me to be with her when she passed to her rest so that she wouldn't feel alone. God gave me exactly what I prayed for. When the time came, I was holding her hand. We sang a few of her favorite hymns.

I told her she was the greatest mom in the world, how much I loved her, and I said, "Ma, if you are tired now and you're ready to go, it's okay, don't try holding on for me. I'll be sad for a while because I *will* **miss you terribly** — but I'll be alright." She squeezed my hand tightly, and then she was gone.

The lost years now seem like a lifetime ago. By the grace and mercy of God, I've been clean and sober for 25 years. I am grateful that God had *another* plan for my life.

God's grace is Him *giving* us what we *don't* deserve, and God's mercy is Him *not giving* us what we *do* deserve.

If *you* want to be free, here's what you can do:

PRAY: "God, please help me. I have sinned, I have been doing my *own* thing, please forgive me, Amen."

And *know* you can speak to God personally anytime, anywhere. *All* He wants from you is to be your Best Friend.

BELIEVE: "God loves *me* and has *another* plan for *my* life." The Bible says in the Book of Mark, Chapter 5, Verse 36, "...Do not fear, only believe."

TRUST: Trust God to keep His word. In the Book of Psalms, Chapter 103, Verse 3 says:

[Say your name here], I (God), have forgiveness for *all* your sins/wrongdoings; I (God), *will heal all* your addictions/illnesses/diseases.

Be Blessed. I will be praying for **you.**

Resources:

Download a free Bible App from the internet, choose a version you can understand, such as New American Standard Bible (NASB).

Website for Bible Studies: www.adventist.org/study-the-bible

Tonya Stokes Ford

Tonya "Tea" Stokes Ford is retired from 29 years of federal government service, ending her career with the Environmental Protection Agency. She is the author of *Left Handers and Right Handers: All of Us Are Clueless.* She is a grandmother to over 40 grand and great-grandchildren. She is a singer and loves music. She now resides in historic and picturesque Washington County, MD.

A believer in continuing education, she is a graduate of the Landmark Education Corporation. "I wouldn't trade my Landmark Education for anything. It touched and still influences my life in profound and unexpected ways."

She recently started an online business as an audiobook publisher. Further details will soon appear on her Facebook page.

Tonya Stokes Ford
8905 Slabtown Road
Hancock, MD 21750
301-648-8077
Stokes4171@gmail.com

Orit Shanet

Stepping into Greatness

So there I was underwater, accepting that my life was over. As I looked towards the light, my entire five years of life flashed before my eyes. I saw my mother, father, and all of my siblings sitting together at the dinner table, smiling at me, saying, "We love you." And all I could think of was, *I love you and goodbye.* Then suddenly, an arm wrapped around me, pulling me up out of the water. As I grabbed onto the wall gasping for air, I glared at the lifeguard and thought, *I almost drowned because of you.* There I was, blaming her for my inability to stay above the water. How silly!! Of course, it wasn't her fault. Yet, at the time, it was easier to blame her than to accept that I was underwater because of me.

Fast forward seven years, there I am waiting in line to take the deep water test so that I could swim in the deep end of the pool. All of my camp friends had been showing off their pink bracelets, so I was determined to get my very own. I mean, there was no way I was going to be the one person who was left out. Yet, there was just one problem — I was petrified. Somehow, by the grace of God, I managed to pass the test. The lifeguard congratulated me and then snapped that prized pink bracelet onto my wrist. As soon as she finished, I showed it to all my friends and let everyone know that I was now a deep-water swimmer. My eyes were shining. I was so happy. I did it!! I got my VERY OWN pink bracelet!! Now that I got that taken care of, there was no way I was actually going to swim in the deep end. So, I came up with a plan. Every day, after putting on my polka-dotted floaties, I'd confidently walk to the deep end of the pool and slide in. I'd then hold onto the wall with both hands, making sure that everyone could see my pink bracelet, and voila, I was a deep water swimmer. It was brilliant. No one would ever suspect that I was scared, and I could still be together with my friends. I had it all figured out, and nothing could ruin it. At least that's what I thought, until one day, this nosy lifeguard decided to challenge me to jump in without my floaties.

"Jump in without my floaties?" I asked, taken aback.

"Yes," said the lifeguard.

I instinctively answered, "No, I can't do that. I'm too scared." The lifeguard looked at me and said, "Well, being able to jump into the deep end is one of the test requirements. If you can't do that, then you are going to have to give back your bracelet."

I looked at her, horrified. *I mean exposing me like that — how could she?*

"What do you mean?" I cried, "I already passed the test, and I swim in the deep every day!"

"Yes!!" she chuckled, "With floaties!!"

I stood there in silence, getting what she was saying.

I looked over at the kiddie pool with all the babies and then looked back at the deep end, where all my friends were. Do I stay in my comfort zone, or do I face my fear head-on? My mind was racing. Yet, there was one thing I knew for sure — there was no way I was going to give up my pink bracelet.

After a few moments, I confidently said, "OK, I'll jump in." As I walked up to the ledge, I instantly regretted ever saying I would do such a thing. Staring at the water, all I could ask myself was, *What if I don't come up? What if I go under and she doesn't save me?* I turned to the lifeguard and asked, "What if I can't do it?"

She smiled at me, "Orit, you already did it. You have your bracelet."

As I looked up at her, she continued, "I know you can do it. Now it's time for YOU to see that YOU can do it."

I suddenly got what she was saying. She was asking me to let go of relying on my floaties. She was asking me to trust myself.

Taking another look at the water, I said to myself, *"I got this. I can do it."* I took a deep breath and jumped. My body hit the water, and I began to sink until my feet touched the floor. I then looked up and saw the light. I said to myself, *Kick.* I started to kick, one foot, then the other foot, and with each kick, I could feel my body being pushed up and up and up, and I could see the light getting closer and closer until my head came up out of the water. I took a deep breath and yelled, "I did it, I did it, Oh my gosh!! I did it!!!" I then turned to the lifeguard and yelled, "I did it, did you see? Woohoo!!" The lifeguard smiled and said, "Yes, you did it! I knew you could do it!" Instantly, I yelled, "I want to do that again!!" I swam out of the water, raced up to the ledge, and jumped in again without hesitation.

That was the day that I learned what it takes to transform, and I'm now going to share that with you.

Be in a Transformational Community

Surround yourself with people who have similar goals and dreams. Find your community and be active in it. Organize a charity event, join a club or volunteer at an organization. Create relationships that bring out the best in you and ask you to step into what's possible. We all need a little push now and then to step out of our comfort zone and into our greatness. True friends encourage us by reflecting on the times where we have already succeeded and illuminate where we can stretch ourselves. They will be at your side, being both a mirror and a light, as you learn and discover yourself.

See, initially, when that lifeguard called me out, I thought, *How dare she expose me like that? She knows I'm terrified. I had this whole thing going for myself, and now she ruined it.* Yet, after I rose to the challenge, I got that she actually gave me a gift of being able to truly discover what I was made of. She challenged me to see that I had already earned that pink bracelet, and so there was no reason to be hanging onto the wall in the way that I was. That day, I learned to trust myself, and I saw that not only could I jump in, but I also loved it.

Be in a Growth Mindset

Be a YES to what's possible for you, take on something big, and play full out to see what you're made of. Start before you are ready. Intentionally stretch yourself and expand your mind by challenging your views. Speak to people from different backgrounds and cultures and learn why they do what they do. Leap outside your comfort zone and take a chance on yourself. Step into your greatness and discover who you truly are. You, too, will get to experience the joy of being able to say, "I did it!!"

When Christie asked if I wanted to be part of this project, I instinctively thought, *No way, I have no idea how to write, and what would I even say? I mean, really, I'm not that interesting.* Yet, regardless of my brain telling me this was a terrible idea, I found my hands signing the contract and handing it in. As I got into the project, I had no idea what I was going to write about, but slowly it came together, piece by piece. It reached the point that I surprised myself with how well I was able to express my ideas through writing. The process taught me that everything looks scarier from the outside, but once you take that first step and get started, it's actually amazing what you get to learn about yourself.

A client shared that after going through a difficult divorce, she chose to stay away from dating. After talking a bit, it became clear that underneath it all, she wanted to be in a relationship yet was simply scared to be heartbroken again. I could hear the pain and the impact that the divorce had on her. I then asked her, "What have you learned about yourself since the divorce?" She went on to share all the growth and lessons that she had learned and then stopped and said, "Wow, I really came far since then." "Yes," I nodded. "So, can you let this new version of you take a chance at love again?" After giving it some thought, she slowly nodded, "Yes." A few weeks later, she called to say that she had started dating again and was so happy that she gave love another chance.

Be in Love with Discovery

Life is a playground. There are new people to meet, swings to play on, and so much to discover. Let out your inner child, stay curious, and take on new adventures. Start a new project, make new friends, or take on a new hobby. Do what you love, let yourself be a student, laugh, make silly faces, and have fun with it. It's OK to be messy. Get some paint on your face, put a flower in your hair, and skip down the street. Be free. Life is magical. Living in discovery allows you to access the joy of life.

A client shared with me that he was looking to improve his relationship with his son but was unsure how. He mentioned that his son created a podcast. So, I asked him if he listened to it. He said, "Na, it's all this gaming stuff. I'm not really into any of that." So, I said, "Ya, but you're into your son, though, right?" He said, "Yes," suddenly paying more attention to what I was saying. So I said, "Your son is telling you about his podcast because he wants to connect with you. By you saying, 'I'm not into gaming,' you're not allowing him to do that with you." He looked at me and said, "Wow, I never saw it that way." The next session, he came back and said, "Not only did I listen to the podcast, I told my son how proud I was of him. I then asked him if he could show me how to play so that we can chill together." He let out a chuckle. "My son was a bit surprised, but I could see it meant a lot to him." He then looked at me and said, "I realized that I wasn't there for my son because I kept telling myself that I'm not good with all this tech stuff, but what I realized is that my son isn't looking for a tech guru, he's looking for a dad."

A few years ago, I was sitting in my room with my friend when she said, "These walls would look so pretty if we painted them a salmon pink color." The next thing I knew, we were both in Home Depot buying paint, rollers, and tape. We somehow managed to get the ladder up and began moving all the furniture around. It was quite a project. I had never painted a room before in my life, and here we were covered in plaster and paint and having a blast. What I learned that day is, it's worth it to take a chance at trying something new. Let yourself get a little messy and not be perfect. What matters is that you went for it and were willing to put yourself out there to learn and discover. Did the walls come out perfect? No, but I got to have a great time with my friend, and I love the new color. When you can embrace experiences as an opportunity to learn something new, then life becomes an exciting adventure.

So, get ready to step into a life that you said yes to and see what's possible.

I invite you to be part of the Masters of Transformation community at www.MastersofTransformation.com, where we embrace our inner child by being young-hearted and passionate students who forever live in discovery. It's going to be fun, powerful, and life-changing as you step into a world where anything is possible!

Orit Shanet

Born and raised in New York, Orit Shanet found her passion for teaching transformative life skills while working at HAFTR High School, guiding teens towards finding their unique path in life. After completing her Bachelor's Degree and Doctorate in Physical Therapy, she discovered that while the body is integral to health and well-being, the key to transformation and accessing new possibilities was created inside of an empowering mindset. Inspiring others to step into their greatness and discover who they truly are, has become her life's work. She is best known for teaching transformative life skills that inspire people to be the heroes of their own stories. Orit founded Masters of Transformation, LLC to provide powerful workshops and private coaching on key topics such as communication, empowerment, and spirituality. Known for her warmhearted, straightforward, and effective approach, Orit empowers others to transform their lives by following their passions, creating meaningful relationships, and stepping into a life that they said yes to.

Orit Shanet

Masters of Transformation

Orit@MastersofTransformation.com

www.MastersofTransformation.com

Game On Plan

Connect with Orit by visiting her Masters of Transformation website at www.MastersofTransformation.com, and download her free "Game-On Plan," which includes five GAME-CHANGING tools to help people get unstuck and live out their wildest dreams.

www.MastersofTransformation.com

Sandra Dugan

My Energetic Awakening

I was 36 years old when my older sister passed. She had fought a drawn-out battle with cancer until she could fight no more. She died in my mother's home in Connecticut. I was living in Canada at the time.

Her illness and subsequent death sent me on a journey of discovery that I could never have guessed I would take. **I needed answers.** My heart was breaking over her ordeal. Because our mother was so angry and frightened, all my access to her was guarded by a wall of denial.

It Was as if It Were Calling Me.

Daily life for me remained largely unchanged because I had my own daughter to raise. Saturday chores needed to be done. One Saturday, as we were enjoying our regularly scheduled trip to Sam's Club, I had *one of the first of many experiences of an energetic intervention.* As we meandered through the aisles, looking at all the offerings we needed, and some we did not, I was drawn to a table full of books. Every time I was within 10 feet of the table, my eye was drawn to the same book.

The book was James Redfield's *Celestine Prophecy.* I heeded the call and bought the book. What I got was a completely different way to look at life and another way to look at death. My feet were firmly planted on the path of energetic exploration.

It Was One of Those Moments That Will Stay With Me Forever.

I was sitting on the deck on our little carriage house in the middle of 35 acres of hardwood trees. I had a cup of tea and a blanket wrapped around me.

The sun was warm, but it was early spring. There was still a chill in the air. There was a small maple tree that the deck had been wrapped around. The sap was just beginning to run, and the squirrels were happily licking the sweetness off the bark. Jake, my German Shepherd, was ignoring them completely while he napped in a warm spot of sun.

I took a deep breath and opened the book. In that moment, I was completely content and ready to dive into whatever *The Celestine Prophecy* had to offer. As I began to read what appeared to be a quick adventure story, certain ideas began to ring true to me. Ideas about how the universe will conspire to make your path more accessible to you. All those times I knew without knowing how or why I knew became clearer to me. The realization that we are all connected energetically was all-consuming for me at that point.

We are all Connected Energetically.

The day my sister died confirmed our connection beyond any reasonable doubt for me. We were not exactly close. We got along well enough, but we were not two peas in a pod by any means. My husband and I had spent the day at the local amusement park with the kids. It was an enjoyable day. Everyone had a fun time. The kids were pretty worn out when we headed home in the evening. I remember reaching across the front seat to touch my husband's arm, and I told him that she was gone. We had been home a few hours when my dad called to tell me she had passed.

It's not that I was oblivious to the pain my parents were in at the time. I didn't react with the extreme grief they were looking for, though. I experienced this event from a completely different perspective than they were experiencing. For me, she was out of pain and rejoining the divine energy we all came from. *She wasn't gone. She took a different shape. She no longer had a corporeal body. She was light. I basked in that.* Even though I was still sad, and I miss her to this day, my heart was also full of love and gratitude for the time she had spent on this planet with me.

Crystals Can Influence Our Energy.

During this same period, I discovered how crystals can influence our energy as well as the universal guidance we receive. I had a friend in Canada who was headed back to the States to appear in court for a rather messy divorce. I was frantic, wondering what I could do for him in this very unsettling time. The day he was heading for the airport, it occurred to me that there was a shop not far from my home that sold crystals, among other things.

I must have looked like a madwoman as I ran into the store that day, just before he left for the airport. I didn't know exactly what I was looking for or what I was supposed to do with it, but I knew it was there. A kind woman asked if she could help me. So, I told her what I knew. I had a friend about to face a difficult situation, and there was something in her shop that could help. We walked over to a glass case, and the only thing I saw was a bag of amethyst runes. I didn't know anything about runes or amethyst, for that matter, but I knew that was what I was there for.

I purchased the runes and headed back to drive my friend to the airport. I handed him the bags of crystals and told him to keep them with him. Much to my surprise, he did. He took the bag, thanked me, and slipped them into his pocket. When we last spoke many years later, and many years ago, he was still keeping them with him.

Spirit Has Guided Me Back.

That perspective has been my guiding force ever since. As often as I have strayed from the healing work I believe I'm here to do, spirit has guided me back. My experiences in Canada were perhaps a little extreme. I was searching at that point and more open to hearing the calling at that point. Even gentle nudges became a magnetic attraction.

As time went on, the reasons I had used to justify my absence from the medical arena became less valid. I had immersed myself in having a more predictable schedule and income in corporate America. I administered health plans and worker's compensation. There were no emergencies that required my presence before or after normal hours. It worked well for a time.

And Then the Universe Threw a Deer at Me.

I am saying that in a very literal sense. I was driving to work early one crisp fall morning. Work was a place with a decent paycheck that I hated going to daily. *I was miserable.*

We lived out in the country, and three does ran across the road in front of me. I immediately looked for the buck that was no doubt following them. There he was, in the ditch beside the road. He was a magnificent 10- or 12-point buck. I stopped the car.

He stood there, letting me admire him for several minutes. To this day, I believe we made eye contact. He didn't move, though. I very slowly started to roll forward and swung into the other lane. (It was very early, and there was no traffic.) That's when he decided to make his point abundantly clear and body slam the car. Then he very casually looked at me and sauntered off after the girls. When I was sure he had no plans to repeat his performance, I continued to make my way to work.

Upon arrival at work, I took note of the damage to the car. There were scratches across the hood of my car where his antlers had been and distinct indentations where his shoulder and bum hit the car. *He had deliberately thrown himself at the car!* I am very grateful it was a big, old Buick, so I wasn't hurt.

A Sign From the Universe.

I took this as a sign from the universe that I needed to do something to make myself happy again. The stag represents masculine energy in ancient traditions. Both Native American and Celtic come immediately to mind. This masculine energy is what propels us forward to make changes in our lives. That's exactly what I did. Within a matter of weeks, I had enrolled in massage therapy school and started classes.

Massage therapy school was just the catalyst I needed to remember what I am here to do. *Healing, for me, is nothing short of magic.* I found myself thrown into a world where people believed the way I do. I met a wonderful young woman who had been so brutalized in her youth that without an energetic connection, no one could touch her. I connected with her, and we learned amazing things about energy from each other. We are still close friends 20 years later.

The years that followed have continued to remind me that our connection is so much stronger than anyone fully realizes. I had known when there was no reason for me to know. I have crossed paths with many wonderful teachers. I have been blessed to work with some of the finest people to walk this planet. That chilly spring day on the deck in Canada began a journey of discovery that, I expect, will continue.

The World is Full of Magic.

One of my newer passions is quantum physics. I thank Gary Zukav and *The Dancing Wu Li Masters* for that. Another book that called my name one day. I believe that the world is full of magic, but I also like to understand the science behind the magic. Discussing the magic peppered with the science makes it difficult to ignore that the energy that connects all sentient beings can be channeled and used to help the healing process.

My focus, at this juncture, is the energy work. I've trained in Reiki and Shamanic healing and Hawaiian Temple Massage. I perform a lot of distance healing work these days, thanks to pandemic quarantine. I have also resumed the development of crystal energy and meditation courses. I've found, in my case, that the universe will let me wander off to renew my own energy levels, but it will continually call me back. Fortunately, for all concerned, I do not need a deer to body slam me in order to hear the calling.

I am returning from an extended sabbatical spent on Martha's Vineyard. I love island life. Being surrounded by water and somewhat removed from conventional society gave my soul a chance to heal. The nuclear family I grew up with have all crossed over to the light. I miss them all but have experienced a softening from judgment and negativity. This has also propelled me forward with my healing work.

The Future Is Not Yet Written.

We all grow and change. This is not always easy on the people who love us and are loved by us. The key is for all of us to allow others the space to make the changes that are so important to fulfilling our mission here in this lifetime. It's a tall order, but we can only move forward with growth, and *growth is often uncomfortable.*

In these times of violence, uncertainty, and universal separateness, we seem to have forgotten how interconnected we all are. These are the times when compassion must become the forefront of our existence on this planet. It is my intention to hold space for us to remember our true nature, which I believe is compassionate kindness, for ourselves, for all sentient beings, and for our planet. We can no longer be passive in our practice of compassion.

The mission of Energetic Essence is to provide energetic support for an awakening planet. We all need to connect with our energetic tribe from time to time. Through individual healing sessions or writing content to reach a larger audience, Energetic Essence will be present to support the effort. *We are all part of a greater web.*

Sandra Dugan

Sandra's path started in the most ordinary way. She grew up in a small family, graduated from high school, and began her service in the US Navy. She wanted to fly fighter jets at the time. It was the 1970's, however, and women just weren't allowed to do that. So, with a big sigh, she became a Navy corpsman. This would turn out to be the moment she found her passion for helping people to heal from sometimes horrific injuries. She also found her calling to teach others the ins and outs of her field.

As time went on, Sandra found her way into the private sector as a medical assistant. Her skill in patient care was enhanced by her ability to relate to the patient and help them express their concerns more effectively to the doctors. She was, in fact, reading their energetic body and helping to translate that into medical jargon.

As her career grew, Sandra found herself working in corporate America designing, communicating, and administering benefit plans. As time went on, her path led back to a more patient care-oriented calling. She attended the Soma Institute in Chicago, IL, where she learned the ins and outs of clinical massage therapy.

As a national board-certified massage therapist, Sandra found her empathic talents coming to the forefront of her life. She completed training to hone her empathic and energetic healing skills.

Sandra is the founder of Energetic Essence, an organization designed to merge her two greatest passions, healing arts, and the written word. Sandra is a Reiki Master Practitioner and has been trained in Shamanism, Qi Gong and clinical massage therapy. She believes that no one travels your healing path for you. However, you may encounter many who will help you along the way.

Sandra is currently designing programs in energy work, crystal healing, and the power of the universe. You can reach out to her at Sandra@EnergeticEssence.net for further information and assistance.

"The greatest tragedy of human existence is the illusion of separateness."
—Albert Einstein

Sandra Dugan
Sandra@EnergeticEssence.net
www.EnergeticEssence.net

THE OVERCOMING MEDIOCRITY

PODCAST with christie ruffino

Each episode features today's top influencers and entrepreneurs on the rise as they share empowering stories and ninja tips meant to become the

FUEL TO IGNITE

a positive change in your life.

Listen on
Apple Podcasts

bit.ly/ompclr

Harness the Power of Story
to Build Your Brand & Attract Clients.

FREE GIFT

Learn how your story can position you
uniquely in the marketplace,
attract clients, and distinguish yourself
from all competition.

OvercomingMediocrity.org/Freebie